Frontispiece

Katsushiki Hokusai
Mount Fuji, Edo period
Smithsonian Institution, Freer Gallery of Art

This Japanese meditation on nature successfully
contrives to bring the observer within the bounds of
the boundless. The man is part of nature,
precariously dependent on her favour, and spiritually
at one with her.

HUX 209 Nature and human nature

IMAGINING NATURE

David Wade Chambers

Deakin University
Victoria 3217
1984

Published by Deakin University, Victoria 3217
First published 1982
Revised edition 1984
Copyright © Deakin University 1984
Edited and designed by Deakin University
Production Unit
Printed by Brown Prior Anderson Pty Ltd

National Library of Australia
Cataloguing-in-publication data

Chambers, David Wade, 1938-
    Imagining nature. Study Guide

    Rev. ed.
    Previous ed: Waurn Ponds, Vic:
    Deakin University, 1982.
    HUX 209.
    Bibliography.
    ISBN 0 7300 0154 7.
    ISBN 0 7300 0132 6. (HUX 209).

    1. Imagery (Psychology). 2. Nature. I. Deakin
    University. School of Humanities. Open Campus
    Program. II. Title. III. Title : Nature and human
    nature.

153.3'2

This book forms part of HUX 209 *Nature and human nature*, a course offered by the School of Humanities in Deakin University's Open Campus Program. *Imagining nature* has been prepared in collaboration with the course team of HUX 209 *Nature and human nature*, whose members are:

David Wade Chambers
Max Charlesworth
Lyndsay Farrell (Chairman)
Allan Johnston
Terry Stokes
David Turnbull

The course includes:
Imagining nature (Study guide)
Imagining nature, Portfolio 1: *Putting nature in order*
Imagining nature, Portfolio 2: *Imagining landscapes*
Imagining nature, Portfolio 3: *Is seeing believing?*
Imagining nature, Portfolio 4: *Beasts and other illusions*

Acknowledgements
We thank all those authors, publishers and other copyright holders who kindly gave permission for the inclusion of material published in this book. While every care has been taken to trace and acknowledge copyright, we tender our apologies for any accidental infringement. We would be pleased to come to a suitable arrangement with the rightful owner in any such case.

NATURE AND HUMAN NATURE

General information on the course

Nature and human nature is a second-level course in the social studies of science major at Deakin University. The course examines a series of scientific ideas and practices, how they were shaped by their social context, and how they were used to further particular social and political ends. In the first half of the course, the focus is on biology since Darwin, in particular on the way in which biological ideas about evolution and heredity have influenced and also reflected their social and cultural contexts. The second half of the course looks at the way in which different cultures have interpreted their relationships with the natural environment.

The course is presented in the form of a number of books which, though based on related themes, may be studied independently. Each book contains full details of prescribed texts and recommended reading. The books also include exercises designed for off-campus students. Students enrolled in the course receive, in addition, audiotapes and other supplementary reading and project materials.

The books in the *Nature and human nature* course are:

Lyndsay Farrall, *Nature and social power*
Rosaleen Love, *Darwin and social Darwinism*
David Turnbull, *Phrenology: the first science of man*
Allan Johnston, *Racism in America*
Richard Gillespie, *Science at work*
Gavan Daws, *The night of the dolphins*
David Wade Chambers, *Imagining nature*
David Wade Chambers, *Putting nature in order*
David Wade Chambers, *Imagining landscapes*
David Wade Chambers, *Is seeing believing?*
David Wade Chambers, *Beasts and other illusions*
Lyndsay Farrall and David Turnbull, *Interpreting the Australian environment*

CONTENTS

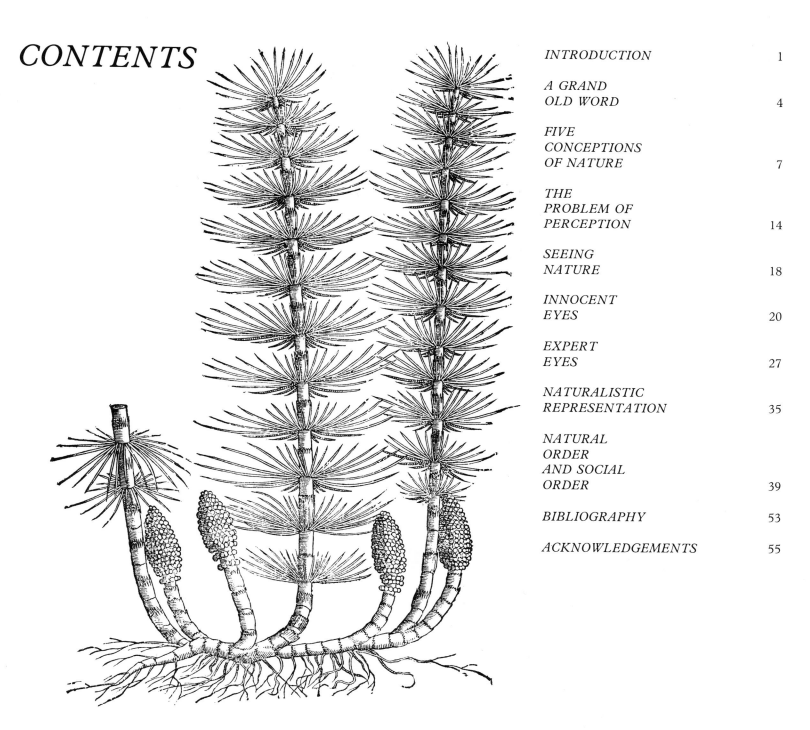

In the matter-of-fact world that we know, the words 'imagination' and 'imagining' have lost much of their quality and have acquired instead a somewhat pejorative meaning, at least in the scientific community. They have come to imply a distorted awareness of reality, often coupled with a lack of intellectual discipline. And yet these words have their origin in one of the most creative characteristics of the human mind – indeed, one of the very few traits differentiating man from higher animals. To 'imagine' clearly means to create an image – more precisely, to select from the countless and amorphous facts and events which impinge upon us a few that each individual can organize into a definite pattern which is meaningful to him. This is what Shelley had in mind when he wrote in *A defence of poetry*, 'We want the creative faculty to imagine that which we know'. To imagine is an act which gives human beings the chance to engage in something akin to creation.

Renē Dubos, *The dreams of reason*, 1961

Casper David Friedrich
The wanderer above the sea of mist, c. 1817
Hamburger Kunsthalle

Here is man, apart from nature and above it, in presumed contemplation of transcendental virtues and vast mysteries.

INTRODUCTION

When we distinguish between seeing and imagining, we usually wish to discriminate between the perception of things 'really there' and the perception of things 'not really there'. So, after reading the title, *Imagining nature,* you may well have expected to encounter the suggestion that some views of nature are imaginary while others are real. In fact no such distinction will be made. Sorting out who sees nature rightly, and who wrongly, is an exercise students may pursue on their own; but after attending to some of the questions raised in this volume, we hope you will begin to doubt the validity of so bald a distinction.

The word 'imagining' is intended to focus discussion on the proposition that all human beings create and imagine nature rather than simply observe and discover it. This is not to deny that observation is our main source of information about the physical world, but to emphasise that observation itself is a subjective interpretive process. The philosophical implications of this thesis, that we actively construct our ideas of nature rather than obtain them through passive observation, will be taken up later.

Because the ideas considered here direct our attention to questions of the relativism of logic and knowledge, it may at times seem to cautious students that one primary objective of the text is the destruction of their belief in universal truths and objective reality. Instead, I hope that each of you will feel encouraged to take any stand you like, or no stand at all, on these weighty philosophical issues. However, if you choose to take a stand, be prepared to support it with considered argument.

The purpose of this book is to help its readers to rethink their ideas of nature: what it means, what it has meant in the past, and what it may come to mean in the future. To this end, ideas and theories are presented from a wide range of thinkers in many academic disciplines and several traditions of thought with the following objectives:

1 to survey a number of possible meanings of the term 'nature';

2 to consider the process by which human beings see the natural world and to explore some of the implications of that seeing;

3 to consider 'nature' and 'culture' as categories of thought, examining some of the difficulties of discriminating between these two closely-related terms;

4 to consider the variety of experiences of nature, including the ways in which different cultures analyse and classify natural objects and natural events;

5 to explore the proposition that all beliefs about nature (even those we call scientific) and all cognitive judgments (even those we believe to be supported by empirical evidence) must be held as provisional and subject to criticism and correction;

6 to enable and assist one to think critically about one's own beliefs about nature as well as the beliefs of others; and

7 to examine the ways in which images of nature interact with social and cultural values and practices.

READING IMAGINING NATURE

This book contains a number of different elements which are described below.

EXERCISES: It is suggested that the reader keep a note-book or journal, for written responses to the exercises.

RESPONSES: One or more possible responses are offered to most exercises. These provide some idea of the kind of answer expected. For most of the exercises there is no one 'correct' response, and often yours will differ from that given. Sometimes your answers may prove 'better' than ours. The main purpose of the exercises and responses is to help focus your thinking.

QUESTIONS TO THINK ABOUT: These questions are designed to stimulate you to formulate some of the fundamental assumptions and significant implications of the material under discussion. Responses are not given in the text but you may wish to make your own notes in your journal.

COMPREHENSION QUESTIONS: Occasionally questions have been included to enable you to check your understanding of points the author considers important. The answer may be easily checked in the preceding text or reading extract.

REFERENCES: Mention is made, both in the main text and in the portfolios, to references which are provided as essential reading. You should read these as directed. Reference 3 IN is also used in later sections of HUX 209. The references are:

1 IN   *Ideas of nature*, by Raymond Williams

2 IN *Phenomenal absolutism and cultural relativism*, by M. H. Segall et al.

3 IN   *African traditional thought and western science*, by Robin Horton

FURTHER READING: At intervals throughout the text issues are raised which you are encouraged to consider more deeply. Further readings are listed to give you an entrée into the area under consideration. You are not expected to consult all the works listed, but rather to follow up those of particular interest to you.

PORTFOLIOS: The material in the portfolios is illustrative of many points made in this volume. You are encouraged to treat the portfolios as if they were exhibits in an art gallery or museum—to be appreciated for their own sake as well as making various points about the way we see nature. Feel free to explore the material in the portfolios before you read this text, *Imagining nature*. Your attention will be directed to specific portfolios as you read this text. All students will be expected to have studied the portfolios carefully by the time this volume is completed.
The portfolios are as follows:

Portfolio 1: *Putting nature in order*

Portfolio 2: *Imagining landscapes*

Portfolio 3: *Is seeing believing?*

Portfolio 4: *Beasts and other illusions*

A GRAND OLD WORD

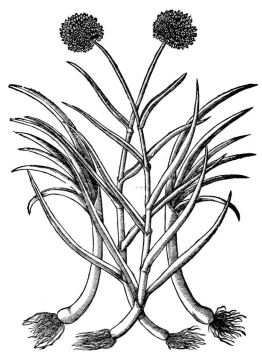

The word 'nature' has many meanings in Greek and Latin and in modern languages. With all its failings it is a grand old word.

Clarence Glacken, *Traces on the Rhodian shore*, 1973

The concept of nature embodies a whole world of ideas. After thousands of years at the centre of Western intellectual discourse, the word itself bears a rich burden of meaning, a fine and sensitive array of interpretation, of subtle and curious usage.

One ecologist claims to have tallied fifty separate meanings for the word. It is not our objective to survey all those meanings and nuances of meaning. Neither would there be any point in trying to find a single magnificent definition which would once and for all delineate the boundaries of what is nature and what is not. Rather let us take a leisured look at some of the more interesting things 'nature' has been taken to mean.

Ideas of nature, and attitudes toward it, are among the most important components of an individual's, indeed of a society's, world view. That is to say, a society's basic beliefs about nature are closely related to that society's values. Nature, or what is thought natural, provides an abundant set of metaphors and analogies that underpin many of our value judgements—what is good or bad, beautiful or ugly, right or wrong.

Through the ages and from culture to culture, region to region, and class to class, fundamental notions of nature have varied quite dramatically. Among people of a particular cultural group there is usually a diversity of ideas about nature, but, in general, members of the same group tend to understand nature in the same way. Indeed, beliefs about nature are often taken as one of the defining characteristics that separate members of one cultural group from another.

EXERCISE

In modern industrial society, despite the various meanings that we attach to the concept of 'nature', we believe we understand it better than it has ever been understood before. On what is this confidence based?

RESPONSE

To a remarkable degree, modern society's claims to understand nature stem from what we call 'science'. For most of us, 'nature' is what is discovered through the study of the natural sciences. The authority of science to determine our understanding of nature has been said to derive from its methods of discovery (observation, experiment, induction, theory construction) and from its procedures for verifying its findings.

Recent thinking in the philosophy of science and the sociology of knowledge has cast doubt upon whether there is such a thing as 'the scientific method' and upon the ability of science to give a true and final picture of nature; yet, however persuasive such arguments may be, they seem unlikely to shake the faith most people hold in scientific institutions. If I am right in this, it is surely because the authority of science in the mind of the average person is based not so much on the picture of nature presented by science as on the power over nature that it is seen to provide. Science gives us a powerful technology—it is the 'engine of progress'—it works, enabling us to make electricity, synthesise drugs, construct machines, etc. On this rock we base our belief that science tells us more about nature than has ever been known before.

Yet there is no *necessary* connection whatever between the truth value of a theory and its instrumental value. For example, Copernican navigators are no better on the high seas than Ptolemaic navigators, and in certain parts of the Pacific both must yield to the Micronesian masters. Our own ability to navigate in space may proceed as much 'in spite of' as 'because of' our theories. To dwellers in the twenty-fifth century our science is likely to appear archaic. Though a little knowledge may be dangerous it may also be useful. Thus, we are right to value knowledge which 'works', but wrong to call that knowledge 'Truth'.

QUESTIONS TO THINK ABOUT

How well do we know nature?

Do we really control it?

How is the understanding of nature related to its control?

If the knowledge which gives us power over nature comes principally from science, we may ask how this power over nature—and how science—is related to political power over human beings.

Is science the only way to know nature?

Are there things about nature that science cannot tell us?

Without benefit of modern science, members of cultures other than those of modern industrial society (e.g. Australian Aboriginal society), have felt great confidence in their understanding of nature and also in their ability to control nature. On what basis would you argue for the superiority of *your* cultural perspective?

EXERCISE

Write down as many meanings of 'nature' as you can think of in 10 minutes.

FURTHER READING

Several classic studies in the history of ideas recount the scholarly particulars of how the concept of nature has changed over the centuries. Studies in the sociology and anthropology of knowledge show how the concept of nature varies from one culture to another.

History of European Ideas

R. G. Collingwood, *The idea of nature*, Clarendon Press, Oxford, 1965.
Clarence H. Glacken, *Traces on the Rhodian shore*, University of California Press, Berkeley, 1973.

Arthur O. Lovejoy, *The great chain of being,* Harvard University Press, Cambridge, Mass., 1964.

Basil Willey, *The eighteenth century background: studies on the idea of nature in the thought of the period,* Chatto and Windus, London, 1967.

Sociology and Anthropology of Knowledge

Barry Barnes, *Scientific knowledge and sociological theory,* Routledge & Kegan Paul, London, 1974.

M. Douglas, *Implicit meanings,* Routledge & Kegan Paul, London, 1978.

R. Horton and R. Finnegan, *Modes of Thought,* Faber and Faber, 1973.

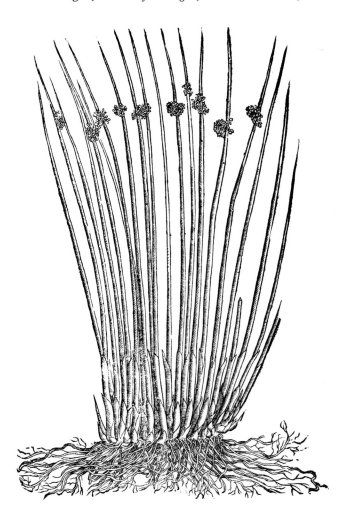

FIVE CONCEPTIONS OF NATURE

Nature as the infinite, unknowable universe

Nature as the material world

Nature as wilderness

Nature as the natural order

Nature as essence

In this section we shall survey five ways of thinking about nature which have been important in the intellectual development of Western civilisation. We do this not only to indicate the diversity of views about nature within modern industrial society, but also to enable comparison and contrast with other cultural perspectives.

NATURE AS THE INFINITE UNKNOWABLE UNIVERSE

All this visible world is but an imperceptible point in the ample bosom of nature. No idea approaches it. In vain we extend our conceptions beyond imaginable spaces: we bring forth but atoms in comparison with the reality of things. It is an infinite sphere, of which the centre is everywhere, the circumferences nowhere. In fine, it is the greatest discernible character of the omnipotence of God that our imagination loses itself in this thought.

Blaise Pascal (1623–1662)

In other words, for Pascal, nature was the entire universe of which our world is a minute and insignificant part, from which the whole can never be understood.

EXERCISE

Does such a concept of nature preclude the idea of scientific understanding? Can one hold such a view of nature and remain a practising scientist?

RESPONSE

Such a view of nature, held by some of the most powerful minds in history, is not strictly incompatible with modern science (when science is seen as a means of providing useful provisional truths), but it does perhaps lead one away from the particular discipline that constitutes the scientific way of investigating things. Pascal himself turned from science to religious thinking and meditation.

QUESTION TO THINK ABOUT

In a society which shared Pascal's vision, what means of shaping and controlling the natural world would be likely to evolve?

NATURE AS THE MATERIAL WORLD

Philosophically considered, the universe is composed of Nature and the Soul. Strictly speaking, therefore, all which philosophy distinguishes as the NOT ME, that is, both nature and art, all other men and my own body, must be ranked under this name, NATURE.

Ralph Waldo Emerson (1803–1882)

This concept of nature, in its purest form, includes the totality of things: all inanimate objects, all life forms, man and all his works, excluding only mental (or spiritual) phenomena.

QUESTIONS TO THINK ABOUT

The mind/body dualism, which Emerson here evokes, divides all the world into mind (or soul) on the one hand, and matter (or nature) on the other. This view, often associated with Descartes, though in fact much older, has had a great influence on Western philosophy and, through it, on Western civilisation. Can you think of some of the implications of this influence? For example, do most people really believe themselves to be part of nature or apart from it? Do you think that you are a part of nature?

NATURE AS WILDERNESS

'Nature', in the common sense, refers to essences unchanged by man; space, the air, the river, the leaf. Art is applied to the mixture of his will with the same things, as in a house, a canal, a statue, a picture. But his operations taken together are so insignificant, a little chipping, baking, patching and washing, that in an impression so grand as that of the world on the human mind, they do not vary the result.

Ralph Waldo Emerson (1803–1882)

This is the meaning of 'nature' most frequently encountered: flowers, forests, oceans, stars; wilderness as opposed to civilisation; pure air as opposed to polluted air; god-given as opposed to man-made; nature (that which is not man-made) opposed to culture (that which is man-made). This view of nature encompasses the three 'kingdoms' — animal, vegetable and mineral — and also includes forces of the natural environment, such as climate and weather. In short, nature is here understood as the ecological system of the planet.

EXERCISE

Emerson, in the mid-nineteenth century, characterised man's operations on nature as 'a little chipping'. In a few words write down your own estimate of mankind's effects on nature. Are these effects great or small? Give examples. Note down viewpoints on these effects that differ from your own.

Philip James de Loutherbourg
An Avalanche in the Alps, c. 1800
The Tate Gallery, London

This terrifying image of nature's overwhelming
might and majesty, and the feebleness of individuals
in her power, is not inconsistent with the idea of
human mastery of the natural world through the
emergence of science and technology.

RESPONSES   1 *Vast effects on nature:* great improvements in such fields as agriculture, medicine, flood control.

2 *Vast effects on nature:* destruction of ecological balance, creation of deserts, extinction of species. The survival of life on Earth threatened on all sides.

3 *Minimal effect on nature:* the ability of nature to resist 'improvement' and to recover from abuse is greater than many realise.

4 *Negligible effect on nature:* even if mankind should utterly destroy the planet Earth, the great universe of nature would not notice. Humanity is nothing in the infinity that is nature.

5 *Nature is irrelevant to humanity:* our relationship with nature is of little consequence, since we have learned to live in a largely synthetic environment.

QUESTIONS TO
THINK ABOUT
Are the above responses mutually contradictory? To what extent do their differences reflect differing concepts of nature?

Can you think of religious, political or economic interests which might determine a person's response to the above exercise? For example, can you predict how a Buddhist's response might differ from that of a fundamentalist Christian; an oil field worker from a conservationist; a supporter of one political party from another?

FURTHER READING
David Wade Chambers, *Liberation and control*, Deakin University, Waurn Ponds, 1979
William Leiss, *The domination of nature*, George Braziller, New York, 1972
Herbert Marcuse, *One dimensional man*, Beacon Press, Boston, 1964
Theodore Roszak, *The making of the counter culture*, Faber & Faber, London, 1972
Lynn White Jr, *Machina ex deo*, MIT Press, Cambridge, Mass., 1968

NATURE AS THE NATURAL ORDER

Unlike the idea of the 'material world', this view excludes culture and all the works of humanity. Unlike the idea of 'wilderness', this view specifically includes, indeed focusses on, the laws, physical forces, and chemical and biological processes that bind the natural world. This is the view that most nearly corresponds to the body of scientific knowledge. Nature here is a category of thought closely aligned with what modern writers consider to be the 'real world': ordered, substantial, even self-evident. Other great categories, such as 'culture', 'society', or 'art', on the contrary, may seem more difficult to pin down, more subjective, perhaps less orderly. In this conception, then, if nature signifies the physical environment, culture might be said to signify human activities and institutions, including our moral and aesthetic values.

NATURE AS
ESSENCE

In the passage below, the distinguished historian, R.G. Collingwood, sets out what was probably the earliest, and what remains one of the most important, meanings of the 'grand old word'.

> When the Ionian physicists asked the question, 'What is nature?' they at once converted it into the question, 'What are things made of?' A modern European, if he were asked the same question 'What is nature?' would be likelier to turn it into the question 'What kinds of things exist in the natural world?' and to answer it by embarking on a descriptive account of the natural world, or natural history. This is because in modern European languages the word, 'nature', is on the whole most often used in a collective sense for the sum total or aggregate of natural things. At the same time, this is not the only sense in which the word is commonly used in modern languages. There is another sense, which we recognize to be its original and, strictly, its proper sense: when it refers not to a collection but to a 'principle'. We say that the nature of ash is to be pliant, the nature of oak to be tough. We say that a man has a quarrelsome or affectionate nature. We say, 'Let dogs delight to bark and bite ... for 'tis their nature too'. Here the word 'nature' refers to something which makes its possessor behave as it does; this source of its behaviour being something within itself: had it been outside it, the behaviour proceeding from it would have been, not 'natural' but due to 'constraint'.
>
> R. G. Collingwood, *The idea of nature*, 1965

These five arbitrary, though hopefully not artificial, definitions of nature may be pushed and pulled, expanded and contracted, separated and conflated to form dozens of interesting, useful and historically valid distinctions. The names we have given the five categories have no particular value except as a shorthand for future reference in this text. The most important point to remember is that 'nature' is an abstraction, one of mankind's oldest ideas: a way of understanding life and death, event and process, order and chaos, the world, the universe.

EXERCISE

One very useful way to understand the meaning of a word is to find other terms with which it may be contrasted, for example, war and peace, good and evil, general and particular, one and many. Nature is endowed with a multitude of 'opposites'. How many can you name? For best results, use the word's adjectival form, 'natural'.

RESPONSE

Contrasting terms for 'natural' include 'unnatural', 'artificial', 'conventional', 'supernatural', 'adulterated', 'affected', 'cultural', 'nurtured', and so on. Several things can be learned from such a list. For example, it may lead us to further meanings of the term nature. Again it shows us how emotionally loaded many of the meanings may be: at least four of the terms listed above have decidedly negative connotations. This observation is important because it helps to confirm the view that it may be misleading to think of nature as a purely factual category, rather than a 'value-laden' one.

EXERCISE · **In social practice, who actually legitimates distinctions between what is natural and what is unnatural?**

RESPONSES · One might suggest priests, judges, medical doctors, legislators, newspaper magnates, scientists, parents, teachers, the ruling class, etc.

We are accustomed to priests and judges assuming the role of moral arbiters, with their respective guides: scriptural injunction and legal codes or conventions. What is often not recognised is that both natural and social scientists make judgements about nature which sometimes have direct, and frequently have indirect, effects in the moral and political spheres. For example, sociologists who describe a particular behaviour pattern as normal, or deviant, contribute to our beliefs about what is natural, what unnatural. Biologists who describe nature as 'red in tooth and claw', or alternatively as characterised by 'mutual aid' may profoundly influence social and political thought.

QUESTION TO THINK ABOUT · Consider the statement 'It is unnatural for a woman to prefer to have a career rather than to have children'. What difference does it make if the speaker is a preacher, a Minister for social welfare, a man commuting to work, or a sociobiologist?

In conclusion, we must emphasise that 'nature' means more than is contained in the five conceptions discussed above. Nature is a house of many mansions, and the meanings that dwell therein, though all of the same family, and a very old family indeed, display to the world a certain non-conformity of usage and emotional colour.

Read Reference 1 IN · In his *Ideas of nature*, reproduced as Reference 1 IN, Raymond Williams traces the history of the consequences of abstracting man from the concept of nature. As you read Williams' essay, note down the changes upon which he focusses.

COMPREHENSION QUESTIONS · What does Williams mean when he says 'the idea of nature . . . contains an extraordinary amount of human history'?

What kind of solution does Williams propose to such vast problems as the alienation of mankind from nature and the ruthless exploitation of nature by man?

EXERCISE · **What are the consequences of holding the view that 'nature' is not a fixed category determined by the real world but rather that it is socially, culturally and historically variable?**

RESPONSE · Judgments about what is natural or unnatural—and especially about the relationship of humanity to nature—can no longer be seen as absolute or certain. Rather they are to be seen as relative to the circumstances in which they are made. To understand that such judgements are problematic, is to allow for their criticism and to encourage the rethinking of human-environmental interaction.

However, to claim simply that 'nature' is a variable concept or a human construction presents a problem; most scientists (and most others) would hold that there is actually something 'out there' that we perceive, even if our understanding of it is of human construction. So let us now consider how we perceive nature and the effects of various influences on that perception.

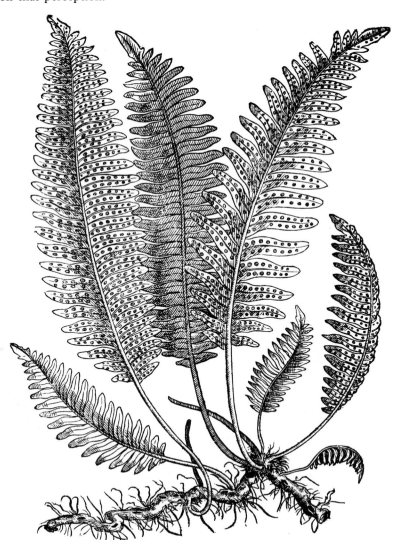

THE PROBLEM OF PERCEPTION

When we say we perceive nature, what is the object of our perception? With reference to the five meanings of nature considered above, we may immediately eliminate the first. By describing nature as beyond our ability even to conceive of, Pascal surely places nature well beyond the limits of sensory perception. The fifth meaning also appears to present a problem since it is often held that the 'essence' of a thing is unknowable because it is unavailable to the senses. However, scientific knowledge goes beyond the senses, postulating theoretical entities and forces (for example, electrons and gravity) which are not observable. On the other hand, many non-industrial cultures have an overriding interest in the essence or spirit of things, knowledge of which they believe to be available—though not necessarily through the senses.

'Seeing nature', in ordinary language usage, is concerned with the third meaning: seeing a country landscape, or birds and flowers—in the purest sense a wilderness. Yet Emerson's reference above, to nature as wild landscapes 'untouched by man', has little meaning in the late twentieth century. Few such places exist now, even in what were once 'remote' parts of the globe. If humans have 'seen' them, then the natural character of these places can not have remained untouched, and indeed has often been completely destroyed. For example, most forests, even those in conservation areas that do not allow logging or mining, must be carefully 'managed'. In these cases human intervention is necessary to preserve ecosystems that have become unbalanced as a result of man's activities whether recreational, agricultural, industrial, military or domestic.

Thus, when we see 'nature' (in the third sense), we see, at best, fragments or, more like-ly, symbolic vestiges of wilderness. Even a single living thing may symbolically represent wilderness, as when a wildflower establishes itself in a crack in a city pavement. That the wilderness ideal remains strong in modern industrial society is shown by the growth in recent years of the environmental movement and by the attempt to preserve a few scattered tracts of the original bush.

QUESTIONS TO THINK ABOUT

If it is true that there is no real wilderness left, in what sense can we talk about nature? How does the absence of environments unchanged by mankind affect our understanding of such contrasts as natural/unnatural, natural/artificial, natural/cultural? What about the contrast between nature and nurture?

The perception of the natural order (our fourth meaning) presents a great many dif-ficulties. In what sense can we be said to perceive the relations of things, the way the world is ordered and subdivided, the forces, objects, processes and laws which we believe constitute and control the physical world of nature? Within this question reside most of the important issues which concern philosophers of science.

Read the first portfolio:
Putting nature in order

The perception of natural order and the extent to which this order may be a product of our own minds has been considered in the first few exhibits of *Putting nature in order*.

Consideration of the perception of 'nature as the material world' (the second meaning) has been saved until last because it provides the best context for introducing a discussion of what we mean by perception itself. (Since the 'material world' may be taken to encompass both 'wilderness' and 'natural order', what is said below about 'seeing' applies equally to the second, third and fourth meanings.) In what respect can we say that we are in contact with the physical world? The clearest answer would seem to be: 'Through our perception of it we see, hear, smell, taste and feel things in our natural environment, establishing that they exist and learning a great many of their physical properties.' Would that we could resolve the matter so easily!

On the surface the matter may seem straightforward enough, yet we run into difficulty whenever we attempt to render a precise account of the relationship of sensory experience to material objects. It is sometimes called the 'problem of perception' and—because seeing is closely related to knowing—forms a major part of what is called the 'problem of knowledge'. In other words, we are touching here on some of the central questions which philosophers have debated through the ages.

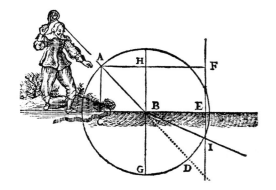

In order to discover something of the essence of the problem of perception, imagine yourself one summer afternoon with a party of your friends lying on the banks of a clear stream in the Snowy Mountains. You see a stick half in the water and half out. Needless to say, you know from experience that the stick, though apparently bent, is actually straight. Later, when a child comes along to disturb your meditation, she sees the stick as bent, and so you patiently explain to her the refractive properties of water. Still later in the day, an English friend comes along to disturb you from what is now clearly slumber. Primed with stories of the deadly snakes that abound in Australia, he suddenly screams that he sees a taipan. When you have calmed him, you are able to explain that taipans are foreign to the region, that he has, in fact, seen a stick half in the water and half out. Toward the end of the afternoon, your profound sleep is interrupted yet a third time by a man, doubtless from another party, standing on the other bank, shaking with delirium tremens and shouting that the water is full of snakes. It would seem fruitless to explain to him that where he is looking there is nothing at all, not even a stick. So you pack up your picnic and return home, reflecting on the four different sorts of perception that have occurred.

1 You saw a stick which you 'knew' to be straight.

2 A child saw the same stick but took it to be bent.

3 A man saw the same stick but took it to be a snake.

4 Where nothing was in the water, another man saw many snakes.

Now, any philosopher worth his salt could have a field day explaining these four instances of seeing, but here it should suffice to make only a few simple points. First,

Joseph Mallord William Turner
Approach to Venice, c. 1843
National Gallery of Art, Washington
Andrew W. Mellon Collection

Duccio di Buoninsegna
The Calling of the Apostles Peter and Andrew,
1308-1311
National Gallery of Art, Washington
Samuel H. Kress Collection

Referring to the Duccio, the Turner and the
Constable (p. 22), Gombrich asks which painting is
truest to nature.

things frequently appear to be different from the way they 'really are'. Alternatively, we might say that the same object may give rise to different, and often conflicting, sense experiences. The fact that in this instance we have ready-made explanations (illusion, expectation, and hallucination) does not change the fact that our sense impressions of objects in the real world are not ultimately reliable.

Philosophers have dealt with this problem in many ways. Some suggest simply that we can have no reliable knowledge of the real world; others say we have no reason even to believe in its existence. Yet others suggest that though we cannot directly perceive external reality, we can establish a causal relationship between external objects and the images, or percepts, formed in our brains.

Another common philosophy distinguishes between the way things appear and the way they actually are. Thus, the notion of 'sense data' is introduced as the name for the appearance of objects we perceive.

> When I see a tomato there is much I can doubt. I can doubt whether it is a tomato that I am seeing, and not a cleverly painted piece of wax. I can doubt whether there is any material thing there at all. Perhaps what I took for a tomato was really a reflection, perhaps I am even the victim of some hallucination. One thing however I cannot doubt; that there exists a red patch of a round and somewhat bulgy shape, standing out from a background of other colour-patches, and having a certain visual depth, and that this whole field of colour is directly present to my consciousness.
>
> H. H. Price, *Perception*, 1932

Another approach accepts that seeing is basically subjective. In this view perceptions should be considered hypotheses about the material world; hypotheses which we may improve, or falsify, by further examining the circumstances of individual perceptions.

It seems that the necessary philosophical argument and/or physiological evidence which would enable the development of a definitive theory of perception has not yet emerged. Since this book is not a treatise, nor even a textbook, in philosophy, we cannot probe the problem of perception as deeply as some might wish; but additional suggestions for further readings in the subject are listed below. Moreover, we can suggest some general conclusions about perception: for example, that perception is not a direct, unmediated process, but an indirect and active one. Further, that nature is a social category embodying at least three aspects: our conceptions of reality, our conceptions of ourselves, and our conceptions of the relationship between ourselves and reality.

FURTHER
READING

John V. Canfield and Franklin H. Donnell, *Readings in the theory of knowledge*, Appleton Century Crofts, New York, 1964 (esp. Part Five, 'Perception', pp. 371–520)
Nicholas Pastore, *Selective history of theories of visual perception: 1650–1950*, Oxford University Press, London, 1971
Godfrey Vasey, *Perception*, The Open University Press, 1973

SEEING NATURE

'The art of seeing nature', said the English painter Constable, 'is a thing almost as much to be acquired as the art of reading the Egyptian hieroglyphs.' (C. R. Leslie, *Memoirs of the life of John Constable*, 1843.) This comment may surprise those readers who are familiar with Constable's own landscapes, which give us a vision of nature which seems simple and true, even obvious, but never hieroglyphic.

Does 'seeing nature' really amount to anything more than opening one's eyes and looking? If an observer's eyesight is intact and if he is honest and not deranged, then surely what is seen depends mainly on what is looked at. Is seeing nature not something we all do equally well, without requiring any special talent or skill and without being greatly influenced by psychological or cultural perspectives?

In this section we shall consider the proposition that the process of seeing involves more than just opening the eyes. To start with a fairly obvious point, artistic or scientific training may enable an observer to discern complexities and relations that would escape an untrained eye. For example, anyone who has walked through the forest with a naturalist knows that one can learn to 'read the woods'. The damaged bark on a tree, a faint sound, a few scratchings in the earth, a flash of yellow wing overhead: these are nature's hieroglyphs. In a scientific laboratory a very different set of hieroglyphic figures are read in the effort to understand nature: litmus turning blue, the temperature of a chemical reaction, an electron micrograph of the structure of a cell membrane.

EXERCISE

Other books published by Deakin University, both in this course and in the *Knowledge and power* series, have examined how social influences such as the specialised training undertaken by scientists affect the generation of scientific theory and help to determine what is accepted as scientific truth. In the light of such considerations, can we say that proficiency in the application of scientific method enables one to see nature more accurately than would otherwise be possible?

RESPONSE

Scientists may or may not see nature better than other people. It depends on what criteria one chooses to apply. Science is sometimes called a 'way of knowing'. For our purposes it might be more appropriately called a 'way of seeing that leads to a particular kind of knowledge'. How closely that knowledge resembles the reality of nature is of course completely beyond the scope of this discussion and, many would argue, beyond the scope of homo sapiens. One pragmatic answer to this question is to say that scientific ways of seeing are useful for many purposes, essential for some, and useless for others.

FURTHER
READING

David Wade Chambers, *On the social analysis of science*, Deakin University, Waurn
    Ponds, 1979
Lyndsay Farrall, *Nature and social power*, Deakin University, Waurn Ponds, 1982

This discussion has not really explained yet what Constable meant when he likened
nature to an Egyptian hieroglyphic inscription. Consider again the evidence of his
landscapes: their strength is found neither in the wealth of natural detail nor in the new
definition of relationships. It is the apparent 'innocence' of vision, the simple mastery of
natural appearance, that signals the genius of a work such as *Wivenhoe Park, Essex*
(1830).

Or so it seems to us now; but in the context of the early nineteenth century, Constable's
view of nature was revolutionary and hard-won. Before Constable, no artist had seen
nature in this way—a way which now seems so plain, straightforward and
unproblematic. Moreover, though his influence in the history of art has been great, no
artist since Constable has seen nature in precisely the way that he did.

One of the most interesting lessons we can learn from the history of art, or even from
the history of photography, or for that matter from the history of science, is that there
is no 'innocent eye'. All human seeing is through 'lenses' that have not only biological
but cultural and psychological tints as well. It is through these lenses that we see nature.

Read the
second portfolio:
Imagining landscapes

I do not mean to say that they distort our vision of the reality of nature, but rather that
they give us the only vision of nature we can have. These 'lenses' (biological,
psychological and cultural) create the images of nature to which we are so emotionally
and intellectually committed.

Yet seeing is not a passive process, as might seem to be implied in the use of the
metaphor of the lens. The many ways in which we as human beings participate in the
process of 'seeing nature' will be explored in the following pages, and especially in the
accompanying portfolios.

Now we turn to the question of how human beings in general perceive and structure the
natural environment. The portfolios provide detailed exemplification which should both
clarify and strengthen the argument developed here.

INNOCENT EYES

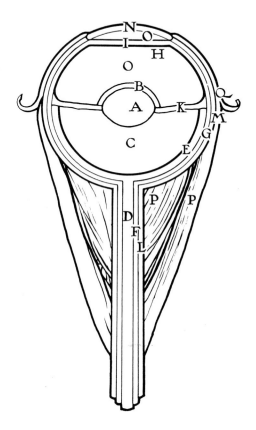

The existence of cultural and psychological dimensions in human perception of the natural world has long been recognised. Curiously, such dimensions are often felt to be needless accretions that distort or otherwise obscure the process of seeing. Could we but recapture the innocence of the child's eye, it is thought, before it underwent social and cultural conditioning, then our vision would be cleansed and our perceptions unalloyed.

This idea of the 'innocent eye' has a long history. John Locke, in the seventeenth century, and George Berkeley, in the eighteenth, speculated on what would actually be seen by a man 'born blind, and afterwards, when grown up, made to see'. (Berkeley, *The theory of vision vindicated*, 1733.) Would he, for example, through sight alone, be able to distinguish between objects, such as a cube and a sphere, which he had previously known only through touch? Locke and Berkeley thought he would not.

The view that receives the most general assent among philosophers and psychologists today holds that seeing is at least in part a learned faculty. The newly sighted man, and indeed the newborn baby, must learn how to see. Berkeley's influential theory asserted that all the eye really sees (that is to say, the only direct object of our vision):

> . . . is light, in all its modes and variations, various colours in kind, in degree, in quantity; some lively, others faint; more of some and less of others; various in their bounds and limits; various in their order and situation.
>
> George Berkeley, *The theory of vision vindicated*, 1733

Our mind then weaves this patchwork of line and colour into a coherent image, based on previous knowledge and experience.

More than one hundred years after the death of Bishop Berkeley, the art historian John Ruskin drew from Berkeley's account the conclusion that painters, wishing to depict nature as it is, should attempt to throw off the knowledge and experience which inform the process of seeing. Ruskin wrote: 'The whole technical power of painting depends on our recovery of what may be called the innocence of the eye.' (*The elements of drawing*, 1857) He enjoined artists to see colours 'as a blind man would see them if suddenly gifted with sight'. This line of thought was extraordinarily stimulating to a number of painters, not least of all the French impressionists, whose canvasses focus our attention on light and shadow, colour, dazzle, and fog. Yet, as convincing as we find the work of the impressionists, we may legitimately question their ability to see with innocent eyes. As Gombrich suggests: 'The innocent eye is a myth. That blind man of Ruskin's who suddenly gains sight does not see the world as a painting by Turner or Monet . . . ' (E. H. Gombrich, *Art and illusion*, 1960).

QUESTIONS
TO THINK
ABOUT

Do you believe it possible for a person to rid himself of the cultural and intellectual associations of seeing?

If attainable, what would be the value of this 'innocent seeing'?

If it is possible to form 'innocent' images of the world, then can one assign meaning to them without re-introducing cultural and psychological parameters'?

Consider the practical difficulties of distinguishing between an art based on 'what is really seen' and an art based on factors other than the strictly perceptual. Is such a distinction possible in practice?

These speculations suggest a number of empirical tests that might be performed. Beginning in the nineteenth century with the great physiologist, Helmholtz, students of perception conceived a host of interesting experiments, whose results are still much discussed. Much work has been done in the study of the fundamental sensory and cognitive aspects of perception and of the role of image formation in both verbal and visual learning.

Accepting the distinction between retinal images and images formed in the brain, we may ask: what does the human mind contribute to the process of seeing? Further, accepting the distinction between innate and acquired aspects of perception, we may ask: in what sense do we learn to see?

To sustain the 'innocent eye' hypothesis, one must hold that seeing is no more than light radiation impinging on the neural receptors (rods and cones) of the retina inducing electrochemical changes which form nervous impulses that travel to the brain. The brain, in this view, contributes nothing more to seeing than its ability to discriminate among and record the nervous stimuli presented to it. Perceptual learning, then, is nothing more than finer discrimination of, and greater receptivity to, the given variables of physical stimulation. Any other activity of the brain is not seeing, but is imagination, fantasy, elaboration, or interpretation. Sophisticated versions of this theory survive, notably in the school of the psychologist and philosopher J. J. Gibson, but some of the view's inadequacies are indicated in the following passage from a lively and popular account of research on human and animal seeing.

> Experiments have acquainted us with a paradoxical fact: man can see 'correctly' only because of his imagination. The human eye, optically speaking, is a piece of bad workmanship. If the image projected onto the retina by the 'camera'—our eye—were examined by an optician used to high standards, he would be disgusted. There is more blurring at the edges than with a cheap pair of child's binoculars; straight lines look curved, and the outlines fade away under iridescent haloes. Yet man, who makes such high demands on spectacles, cameras, binoculars, and microscopes, does not notice anything at all of the short-comings of his own optical gear: the nervous system corrects these faults so perfectly that we perceive a technically flawless image of our surroundings.
>
> Vitus Droscher, *The magic of the senses*, 1969

John Constable
Wivenhoe Park, Essex, 1816
National Gallery of Art, Washington
Widener Collection

Constable's landscapes give a vision of nature which
seems simple and true, even obvious, but never
hieroglyphic, or so it now seems to us. At the time
his view of nature was revolutionary.

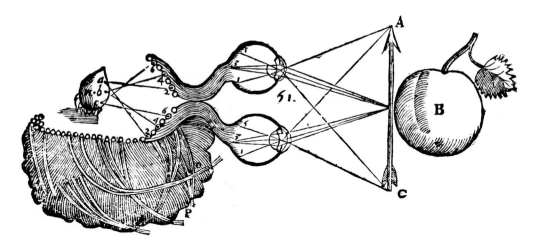

This conclusion had been reached by Dr Anton Hajos of the Institute of Experimental Psychology at Innsbruck University, and further proof was supplied by an exciting series of tests. For days, even weeks, Dr Hajos and his students wore spectacles with badly distorting prismatic lenses. Here is part of his report:

> While the experiment is going on, the subject is condemned exclusively to a world reshaped by prismatic lenses, in which straight lines appear curved, angles are distorted, and sharp outlines seem fringed with colour. Objects are not where the subject thinks he sees them, and they perform ghostly movements as soon as he moves his head; heavy objects seem to skip about when he ventures a few steps. But it does not take long for the grotesque world of the prism victim to appear normal. Gradually the distortions, coloured fringes, and 'apparitions' dwindle, and after about six days the subject recovers his impression of a normal, stable, and optically almost perfect image of his environment. The nervous system has compensated for the conjuring tricks of the spectacles by its processing of the transmitted image. This is not all, how- ever. When the subject takes off his prismatic glasses, the world once more appears to him as if reflected in comic distorting mirrors—except that now the straight lines curve the other way, and outlines are blurred by the opposite colours.
>
> Vitus Droscher, *The magic of the senses*, 1969

A common, if naive way to describe what takes place in human seeing is shown by the following schema:

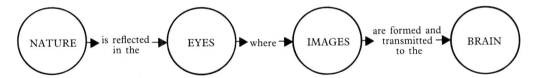

In other words, nature is thought of as the real world, and the eye forms images of the real world which are then transmitted to the brain. We have already indicated some of the inadequacies of this seemingly straightforward account. First, this approach assumes that the actual process of seeing does not actively involve the brain. Second, it is further assumed that what happens is largely unproblematic, dictated exclusively by characteristics of the natural objects seen and the physical laws of optics.

A more sophisticated view might be represented like this:

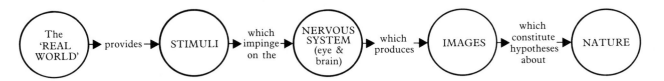

Every stage in this activity deserves, and in recent years has received, close scrutiny.

EXERCISE   **What distinguishes the second schema from the first?**

RESPONSE   The most important difference is that, in the second version nature, as we come to know it, is not 'seen' as a 'given' but is a complex product of nervous activity and mental speculation as to the meaning of stimuli reaching us from the 'real world'.

Though perhaps logically separable, seeing and interpreting are so closely interrelated in life that they must be understood as reflexive elements of a single process. That we are not aware of the continuous necessity to interpret visual stimuli is due to the years of training and experience which enable the brain instantaneously to determine the 'meaning' of familiar incoming signals.

To explore this further, let's take a very simple case. While sitting in the front room of your house, you hear a noise. You walk to the window, look out, and after a few moments say to your companion: 'A Mercedes has stopped in the street.' Of course seeing a car parked in the street is an everyday experience. But let us review the event. You look out of the window and see—what? Through the leafy shrubs you glimpse a movement, then a vague shape, then a distinct outline. From this you identify a car, a Mercedes, noting its colour and perhaps other details.

Ruskin's blind man to whom sight has been restored, or a newborn infant, could not distinguish a car seen momentarily through the shrubs of a garden—or even, indeed, visible without hindrance. Your case, though, is different. You were, after all, half expecting to see a car. You had an aural clue, and have heard and seen many cars before; and the object was in context: 'in the street'.

But how did you know that it was a Mercedes and not a Honda? 'The size of it', might be your first answer. Very well, what was the size of it? And how did you determine the size? You did it, I suggest, by estimating the distance of the object from your eye and through contextual clues. You performed this operation readily through past experience; but you may have missed the subtlety of your performance. For instance, the optical image of a Honda in your driveway is measurably larger than the optical image of a Mercedes out in the street. Based on previously acquired knowledge, your brain correctly reverses the optical information sent along by the retina, and you see the Mercedes as larger.

Again, based on retinal information alone, we would see people increase in stature as they approached and diminish as they departed. However flattering such an interpretation might be, the mind is able to sustain an impression of constant size. Constancy is the name which psychologists give to the ability of the brain to maintain unchanged perceptions of objects in the face of continual changes and ambiguities in the retinal information.

Empirical evidence indicates that relevant experience and contextual stimuli are both essential for the size constancy phenomenon to occur. For example, young children do not experience it at a distance. Thus, Helmholtz remembers as a child at church mistaking people in the belfry for dolls and asking his mother to hand them to him. Similarly, Colin Turnbull recounts a forest-dwelling Congo Pygmy's first encounter with animals on the open plains:

> Kenge . . . saw the buffalo, still grazing lazily several miles away, far down below. He turned to me and said, 'What insects are those?' At first I hardly understood him; then I realised that in the forest the range of vision is so limited that there is no great need to make an automatic allowance for distance when judging size. Out here in the plains, however, Kenge was looking for the first time over apparently unending miles of unfamiliar grasslands, with not a tree worth the name to give him any basis for comparison. . . . .
>
> When I told Kenge that the insects were buffalo, he roared with laughter and told me not to tell such stupid lies. . . . .
>
> The road led on down to within about a half a mile of where the herd was grazing, and as we got closer, the 'insects' must have seemed to get bigger and bigger. . . . I was never able to discover just what . . . [Kenge] thought was happening—whether he thought that the insects were changing into buffalo, or that they were miniature buffalo growing rapidly as we approached. His only comment was that they were not real buffalo, and that he was not going to get out of the car again until we left the park.
>
> Colin M. Turnbull, *The forest people*, 1961

These simple examples demonstrate several points made earlier: that seeing is not a passive process, that the mind contributes significantly to the act of seeing and that the mind, in effect, must learn to see. Much more evidence might be brought to bear on these questions. For example, the concept of constancy may also be shown with regard to colour, brightness and shape.

FURTHER
READING

C. M. Bloomer, *Principles of visual perception*, Van Nostrand Reinhold, New York, 1976

J. J. Gibson, *The perception of the visual world*, Houghton Mifflin, Boston, 1950

E. H. Gombrich, *Art and illusion*, Phaidon Press, London, 1960, (esp. Chapter IX)

R. L. Gregory, *Concepts and mechanisms of perception*, Scribner's Sons, New York, 1974

R. L. Gregory and E. H. Gombrich (eds.), *Illusion in nature and art*, Duckworth, London, 1973

P. K. Machamer and R. G. Turnbull, (eds.) *Studies in perception*, Ohio State University Press, Columbus, 1978

M. J. Morgan, *Molyneux's question*, Cambridge University Press, Cambridge, 1977

Read the third portfolio
Is seeing believing?

EXPERT EYES

Closely related to the 'innocent eye' approach in art history is another kind of explanation of artistic change and diversity: the 'expertise' account. In this view, the history of art becomes a narrative of technical advances in the capacity to draw or paint with naturalistic accuracy. Thus, through a series of inventions of new techniques (such as the Renaissance discovery of perspective), successive artists through the ages accumulate devices and procedures for improving the representation of natural appearances.

Roger Fry, in his book on Constable, *Reflections on British painting* (1934), characterised the history of art as 'the gradual discovery of appearances ... gradually symbolism approximates more and more to actual appearance ... Indeed, it has taken from Neolithic times till the nineteenth century to perfect this discovery.'

EXERCISE

How well do you think this characterisation applies to developments in landscape painting which appeared later in the twentieth century?

RESPONSE

Many of the twentieth-century works which art critics now see as the most important appear to contradict Fry's thesis. With some recent exceptions, symbolism and abstraction have come to dominate naturalism and representationalism. In the terms of the particular quotation from Fry above, the twentieth century might reasonably be seen as an age of decline and decadence in art—though in fact Fry went on to 'hail impressionism as the final discovery of appearances'.

EXERCISE

Both the 'innocent eye' and the 'expertise' theories assume that naturalistic accuracy has been the major aim of artistic development. Is this a valid assumption?

RESPONSE

Accurate depiction of the world of appearances has been one of the objectives which some artists through the centuries have set themselves. Nevertheless, many additional aims must surely be admitted as valid. The things that matter to an artist and his audience have often had to do with the beauty and harmony of forms; an explicit religious or political content; the expression of complex states of mind, and so forth. In the twentieth century, perhaps because so many of the technical difficulties of natural representation seem to have been resolved, these ancillary goals have often come to the fore.

If we try to view art history as nothing more than the struggle to portray the world 'as it really is', we encounter difficulties in every historical period; for realism has frequently not been the only goal, or even the overriding goal of artists.

COMPREHENSION QUESTION

How do the 'innocent eye' and the 'expertise' schools respectively account for historical improvements in artistic efforts to portray the natural world?

The former concentrates on improving the process of seeing nature by removing cultural, religious, aesthetic, and even scientific preconceptions which might corrupt one's direct apprehension of natural form. The latter takes seeing as given and emphasises portraying nature as having advanced through the development of specific techniques. This technical evolution owes much to the advent in Western culture of the sciences of optics, geometry and anatomy. When referring to the way an artist 'sees' nature, writers often conflate the two concepts of seeing and portraying, presumably because the latter is our only evidence of the former. What artists portray is our only evidence of what they see.

In science this conflation is perhaps even more pronounced than in art: scientific descriptions of nature (whether expressed mathematically or verbally) are usually taken to be observations of nature, and indeed are often referred to as such. Furthermore, these 'observations' may themselves be taken to be 'facts', i.e. nature as it really is.

The philosopher of science, N. R. Hanson, has lampooned the suggestion that we can somehow 'see' facts. Only in the light of theories we hold, hypotheses we consider, and languages we speak, are we able to identify certain events or statements as facts:

> Facts? Why they are just the things that happen: the hard, cold, stubborn facts, the sheer, physical, plain, and unvarnished facts, the observable facts out there for all of us to see, come up against, trip over. You know, we face the facts, collect them: the little, detached, lawless, particular, and individual facts. Facts, in short, are just chunks of the material world; sticks, stones, boxes, and bears. Of those of us who so readily speak of observing the facts, looking at them, collecting them, etc. — and most of us do so speak — has anyone ever asked what observation of a fact would be like? What do facts look like? In what receptacle might we collect them? I can photograph objects like X-ray tubes, or events like fluorescence, or situations like the set-up of an X-ray diffraction experiment. But what sort of photograph would a photograph of a fact be? Asking the question in this way is like biting the forbidden apple. Facts can never again be regarded in the fat, dumb, and happy way we looked at them before. It is like discovering of a close friend that he was educated at Oxford or Princeton.
>
> N. R. Hanson, *Perception and discovery*, 1969

Hanson has given us a stimulating and coherent defence of the proposition that 'there is more to seeing than meets the eye', i.e. that the process of seeing is not just retinal activity but involves interpretation, based on the observer's knowledge and experience; 'there is a very intimate relationship between the ways in which we speak and write and the ways in which we think, and between both of these and the ways in which we see the world ' (*Perception and discovery*, 1969).

No student who has studied anatomy can forget the importance of adequate preparation for laboratory dissection. Having read the textbook carefully in advance, you can see the anatomical structures discussed. With no preparation, the relevant structures are often

destroyed before one can even begin to interpret the mass of animal tissue on the tray. The secret is not steady hands but knowing what you are supposed to see.

Similarly in microscopy, prior study enables you to see the expected structures:

> Freshmen were asked to identify and write illustrated notes on specimen X (a tranverse section of hydra). Those who identified X correctly drew what looked much more like textbook drawings of hydra than the specimen before them. Those who failed to identify X produced drawings superior in every respect. Apparently, once having identified X as hydra, and having no reason to doubt this, the student begins to see the specimen through those elusive spectacles he wears behind his eyes, spectacles ground, shaped, and tinted by textbooks and illustrated lectures in invertebrate zoology.
>
> N. R. Hanson, *Perception and discovery*, 1969

The philospher Michael Polanyi introduces us to the way instruction changes a medical student's perceptual experience when he looks at an X-ray picture:

> Think of a medical student attending a course in X-ray diagnosis of pulmonary diseases. He watches,in a darkened room, shadowy traces on a fluorescent screen placed against a patient's chest, and hears the radiologist commenting to his assistants, in technical language, on the significant features of these shadows. At first, the student is completely puzzled. For he can see in the X-ray picture of a chest only the shadows of the heart and ribs, with a few spidery blotches between them. The experts seem to be romancing about figments of their imagination; he can see nothing that they are talking about. Then, as he goes on listening for a few weeks, looking carefully at ever-new pictures of different cases, a tentative understanding will dawn on him; he will gradually forget about the ribs and begin to see the lungs. And eventually, if he perseveres intelligently, a rich panorama of significant details will be revealed to him: of physiological variations and pathological changes, of scars, of chronic infections and signs of acute disease. He has entered a new world. He still sees only a fraction of what the experts can see, but the pictures are definitely making sense now and so do most of the comments made on them.
>
> Michael Polanyi, *Personal knowledge*, 1973

Finally, another philosopher, Pierre Duhem, illustrated graphically the utter inability of an untrained person to see what the physicist sees:

> Enter a laboratory; approach the table crowded with an assortment of apparatus, an electric cell, silk-covered copper wire, small cups of mercury, spools of wire, a mirror mounted on an iron bar; the experimenter is inserting into small openings the metal ends of ebony-headed pins; the iron oscillates, and the mirror attached to it throws a luminous band upon a celluloid scale; the forward-backward motion of this luminous

spot enables the physicist to observe the minute oscillations of the iron bar. But ask him what he is doing. Will he answer 'I am studying the oscillations of an iron bar which carries a mirror'? No, he will answer that he is measuring the electric resistance of the spools. If you are astonished, if you ask him what his words mean, what relation they have with the phenomena he has been observing and which you have noted at the same time as he, he will answer that your question requires a long explanation and that you should take a course in electricity.

Pierre Duhem, *The aim and structure of physical theory*, 1954

Most readers (with or without a scientific background) will be aware of the disciplined training essential for success in science. And, indeed, the philosophers Karl R. Popper and Thomas S. Kuhn, among others, have emphasised the role of instruction and experience in scientific seeing.

However, expectation may lead scientific seeing significantly astray. Scientists who are committed to particular theories may 'see' only the data or results which support those theories. There are a number of historical examples of this. Shortly after the discovery of X-rays the leading French physicist, Blondlot, announced the discovery of what he termed N-rays. Scientists all over France began to observe, under controlled conditions, the various effects of the new phenomenon. A number of noted French scientists published papers on N-rays before it was finally established that N-rays were nothing more than a figment of Blondlot's imagination.

A more recent example is that of Sir Cyril Burt's data concerning the intelligence of identical twins. Burt produced data to support the theory that intelligence is largely determined by heredity. This data was accepted for many years and greatly influenced scientific thinking before it was discovered that it had been fabricated.

EXERCISE **What conclusions would you draw from these examples about the practice of science?**

RESPONSE Firstly, for the lay person, most published scientific data must be accepted on faith, and, curiously enough, most scientists seem no more concerned over this state of affairs than medieval priests asking that divine revelation be accepted on faith. Secondly, social implications of great magnitude result from the ways in which scientists are trained. Consider, for example, the differing ways in which the Great Barrier Reef is seen by marine biologists on the one hand and by petroleum geologists on the other. To put this difference down to differing values is to miss what Kuhn has called 'the essential tension' in science. In order to be able to see the world as a scientist you must acquire the lenses of training and experience which may sharpen focus, but which also distort and blinker. For this training and experience may generate such strong commitments to theories and, consequently, expectations of nature that relevant or even falsifying data may be overlooked or ignored, and false data may be invented.

Samuel Palmer
A Shoreham Garden, c. 1829
Victoria and Albert Museum, London

Frederick McCubbin
The Letter, 1885
Ballarat Fine Art Gallery – City of Ballaarat

Unlike the men who appear in landscape paintings, women are rarely seen as 'apart from nature', distanced observers in meditative or scientific contemplation. Often their presence is given anecdotal justification, as in the McCubbin painting. Alternatively, women are often used as ornamentation of a natural setting, as in the Palmer watercolour in which an ecstatic joy in the natural world is focussed on a feminine form in the distance.

FURTHER
READING
Stephen Jay Gould, *The mismeasure of man,* Norton, New York, 1981

N. R. Hanson, *Patterns of discovery,* Cambridge University Press, Cambridge, U.K., 1958

N. R. Hanson, *Perception and discovery,* Freeman and Cooper, San Francisco, 1969

Liam Hudson, *The cult of the fact,* Jonathan Cape, London, 1972

QUESTION
TO THINK
ABOUT
Accurate depiction of the natural world is an aim of both science and art. What are the similarities and differences in the two traditions?

OPTIONAL
ESSAY
PROJECT
E. H. Gombrich's *Art and illusion* (1960) re-interprets the history of visual discovery in the world of art as a project process of 'making and matching', of 'schema and correction'. His theory deliberately applies Popper's epistemology to the history of art:

> . . . the nineteenth century believed in passive recording, in unbiased observation of uninterpreted facts. The technical term for this outlook is the belief in induction, the belief that the patient collection of one instance after the other will gradually build up into a correct image of nature, provided always that no observation is ever coloured by subjective bias. In this view nothing is more harmful to the scientist than a preconceived notion, a hypothesis, or an expectation which may adulterate his results. Science is a record of facts, and all knowledge is trustworthy only in so far as it stems directly from sensory data. This inductivist ideal of pure observation has proved a mirage in science no less than in art. The very idea that it should be possible to observe without expectation, that you can make your mind an innocent blank on which nature will record its secrets, has come in for strong criticism. Every observation, as Karl Popper has stressed, is a result of a question we ask nature, and every question implies a tentative hypothesis. We look for something because our hypothesis makes us expect certain results. Let us see if they follow. If not, we must revise our hypothesis and try again to test it against observation as rigorously as we can; we do that by trying to disprove it, and the hypothesis that survives that winnowing process is the one we feel entitled to hold, pro tempore.
>
> E.H.Gombrich, *Art and illusion,* 1960

In one of those interesting examples of the interactions between the understanding of art and science, Gombrich's Popperian approach served as a basis for Kuhn's theory of the development of science. If you choose to write this essay project, then you are asked to compare and critically review the theories of Gombrich and Popper. You may also wish to include a comparison of Gombrich's notion of schema with Kuhn's idea of the paradigm.

SUGGESTED
READING FOR
OPTIONAL
ESSAY
Allan Chalmers, *What is this thing called science?* Queensland University Press, Brisbane, 1979

Max Charlesworth, *Science, non-science and pseudo-science,* Deakin University, Waurn Ponds, 1982

E.H. Gombrich, *Art and illusion,* Phaidon Press, London, 1960

T. S. Kuhn, *The structure of scientific revolutions*, University of Chicago Press, 1970

T. S. Kuhn, *The essential tension*, University of Chicago Press, 1977

Karl, R. Popper, *The logic of scientific discovery*, Hutchinson, London, 1972

Karl, R. Popper, *Conjectures and refutations*, Routledge and Kegan Paul, London, 1972

Richard Wollheim, 'Reflections on Art and illusion', in Richard Wollheim, *On art and mind: Essays and lectures*, Allen Lane, London, 1973, pp. 261–289

In the same lecture (given at the Royal Institution in 1836) in which John Constable compared seeing nature to reading hieroglyphics, he also remarked:

> Painting is a science, and should be pursued as an inquiry into the laws of nature. Why, then, may not landscape painting be considered a branch of natural philosophy [we would say physics] of which pictures are but experiments?
>
> C. R. Leslie, *Memoirs of the life of John Constable*, 1843

If Constable saw both art and science through the eyes of inductivist philosophers, Gombrich sees them both through Popperian eyes. Whatever one's philosophical overview, we have found interesting similarities between the methods used in art and in science to see and portray the world of nature. In both, mechanisms and techniques have been developed to facilitate attempts to see the world through expert eyes and to improve the accuracy of their descriptions of it.

EXERCISE

With reference to the 'innocent eye' and the 'expertise' theories, how do art and science differ?

RESPONSE

One important difference may be found in artistic acceptance of the individual authenticity of perception contrasted with scientific insistence on consensus and replication of results. Yet this contrast may have been overemphasised. In art consensus of the critics and in the market place count for much.

In addition to 'innocent eye' and 'expertise' explanations of the great diversity we find in naturalistic art, there is a third approach we may call 'relativism'* in which, as characterised by its critic Wollheim:

*These three approaches while corresponding in some respects to actual threads in the weave of history, have been isolated here, and arbitrarily named, only to facilitate the present discussion.

> . . . each painter paints the world as he sees it, but each painter sees the world for himself, idiosyncratically, so that the various manifestations of representational art can be accounted for in terms of the varieties of human perception.
>
> R. Wolheim, *On Art and mind*, 1973

While none of these views can be accepted uncritically, each can contribute to our understanding of how we (as artists, scientists, and laypersons) see the natural environment. The 'innocent eye' notion correctly holds that our intellectual presuppositions affect the way in which we see. The naivety of this approach lies in the suggestion that we can and should rid ourselves of fundamental cultural commitments and that we can eventually see the world without preconceptions.

The 'expertise' idea points to undoubted improvements in our capacity to communicate images of the structure and complexity which we attribute to nature, but tells us little or nothing of the process of seeing itself. Furthermore, art history when viewed merely as advancing expertise ignores human values and is unable to explain, for instance, why some people may aesthetically prefer, say, the cave drawings of prehistoric Europe to the paintings of the impressionists, or the art of the Quattrocento to that of the twentieth century. E. H. Gombrich (*Art and illusion*, 1960) drives this point home by noting that 'even the crude coloured renderings we find on a box of breakfast cereal would have made Giotto's contemporaries gasp.' However, acknowledging 'the victory and vulgarisation of representational skills' does not oblige us to conclude that 'the box is superior to a Giotto.'

The 'relativist theory', because of its emphasis on the authentic diversity of human vision has most to offer us in our deliberations here. If we accept that cultural, linguistic, geographical, familial, and psychological considerations shape the way we see the world, then we can not only explain the fact that the history of art displays incredible diversity, but we can also begin to account for such issues as the coherence of cultural traditions, the existence of regional affinities and the evolution of an individual's style over time.

Much more of interest might be said on behalf of or in objection to these three approaches; however we turn now to a question that is central to this discussion no matter what one's theoretical perspective.

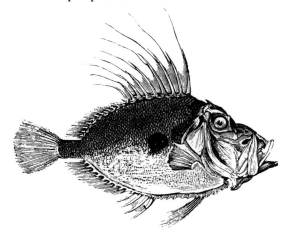

NATURALISTIC REPRESENTATION

EXERCISE

Given the embarrassing diversity of human attempts to portray the world precisely as it looks, we may be forgiven for posing a fundamental question: is naturalism in art ever possible?

RESPONSE

Commonsense supplies us with an immediate answer: yes, of course it is. If we cannot assert that one painting, say by Constable, is more naturalistic than another, say by Picasso, then we can know nothing about nature at all. If naturalistic representation were completely impossible then how could we begin to explain the recognition of natural subjects in art? For example, in the woodcut above which depicts horses at a race track, any person familiar with horses can recognise the animal for what it is.

If naturalism is taken to mean effective imitation of natural objects, then the first naturalistic artist was nature herself. This is no paradox: consider the biological phenomena of mimicry and camouflage: twig-like caterpillars, leaf-like insects, and owls that appear to be bumps on a log. These likenesses are realistic enough to fool not only human eyes, but also the remarkably varied and often keener vision of predators. However, there are extreme statements of the naturalism thesis, which are far more dubious. For instance, an 'innocent eye' interpretation suggests that a truly naturalistic canvas is one in which sensory input alone determines every brush stroke; one in which there is a direct and precise equivalence between retinal image and artistic presentation. By this interpretation there can be one, and only one, true portrayal of a particular object or scene.

In denying this position (which he calls 'neutral naturalism'), E. H. Gombrich assembles an array of arguments which surely disprove the notion once and for all. One line of his argument (here recapitulated by his stern critic and admirer Richard Wollheim) goes as follows:

> . . . though certain forms of art are clearly non-naturalistic, there is no unique form of naturalistic art towards which all forms of representational painting approximate to a greater or lesser degree. To posit the existence of such a style would be to make two

further assumptions. First, that the conveying of information is a simple cumulative task, so that a picture containing a certain amount of information could always be revised so as to convey some further piece of information. But it may be that some information can be conveyed only at the expense of omitting other information: in constructing a picture we may have to make a choice. Indeed, Gombrich points out not merely that this may be so, but that in fact it is so—and he illustrates his point ingeniously by comparing three representations of a boat, one by Duccio, one by Constable and one by Turner, and he shows how, as we cast our eye across the paintings in historical sequence, we get progressively more information about the appearance of the boat as at a certain moment and in a certain light, and progressively less information about the structure of the boat. We are told new things at the price of having to take familiar things for granted.

See pp. 16 and 22

R. Wollheim, *On art and mind*, 1973

Very different pictures might emerge from two 'equally naturalistic' painters attempting to portray the same scene because, unable to convey all the information encountered, each would have to select what was to be included and what left out. Which painting then could be said to represent the actual appearance of the scene?

Every individual (artist or non-artist) who perceives a particular natural landscape notices some things and fails to notice others, attaches greater significance to some things than to others, remembers some things and forgets others. Even a supposed 'innocent eye' would necessarily engage in this highly subjective activity of selecting which information to record. This same process of selection goes on in science as well as art, and its importance has been stressed by philosophers such as Karl Popper and scientists such as the theoretical physicist Erwin Schrodinger.

It must also be pointed out that the test of 'recognition' earlier proposed in connection with the naturalism of the woodcut on page 35 is of no avail in establishing the extreme version of the naturalism thesis. While these animals may be universally recognised as horses, they may actually convey false information. In a gallop all four of a horse's hooves are never fully extended at the same time. This fact of locomotion was apparently missed for thousands of years in both East and West.

But, what about photography? Can we say the camera gives us direct access to nature in a way the human eye cannot? Gombrich takes up this point:

Historians of art have explored the regions where Cézanne and van Gogh set up their easels and have photographed their motifs. Such comparisons will always retain their fascination since they almost allow us to look over the artist's shoulder—and who does not wish he had this privilege? But however instructive such confrontations may be when handled with care, ... [s]hould we believe the photograph represents the 'objective truth' while the painting records the artist's subjective vision—the way he transformed 'what he saw'? Can we here compare 'the image on the retina' with the 'image in the mind'? Such speculations easily lead into a morass of un-provables. Take the image on the artist's retina. It sounds scientific enough, but actually there never was one such image which we could single out for comparison with either photograph or painting. What there was was an endless succession of innumerable images as the painter scanned the landscape in front of him, and these images sent a complex pattern of impulses through the optic nerves to his brain. Even the artist knew nothing of these events, and we know even less. How far the picture that formed in his mind corresponded to or deviated from the photograph it is even less profitable to ask.

E. H. Gombrich, *Art and Illusion*, 1960

Can you think of other evidence than that presented by Gombrich that even the camera does not give us an innocent image? In the final analysis, is photography a more 'objective' way of seeing than the human eye?

There is a basic defect in the latter question since we can only see photographs with our own eyes. Leaving that objection aside, one might also point out that the camera places a technological system between the observer and the observed. Isn't it always better to see an object or an event directly rather than merely to see a picture of it? After all, the larger context may be missed by the camera.

On the other hand, at the time of its invention, there quickly developed an awareness that the camera was more than just a 'memory device' for recording seen images. Such early photographers as Daguerre and Fox Talbot 'thought of photography as a kind of collaboration with nature, a means whereby natural forces could be allowed to speak for themselves, instead of having to filter their message through the individual temperament' (E. Lucie-Smith, *The invented eye*, 1975). Indeed, Fox Talbot chose to call his book on photography *The pencil of nature.*

If photography cannot honestly be called nature's pencil, it is nonetheless true that the camera reveals aspects of nature which the eye had not previously seen. That the camera in certain respects radically revised how we see nature is best illustrated perhaps by Eadweard Muybridge's photographic recording, in the late nineteenth century, of animal movement (*Animals in motion*, reprinted 1957). These pictures demonstrated, incidentally, the actual motion of the horses' gallop which naturalistic painters had missed.

But is the full truth revealed by freezing one moment in time? Ultimately, as any modern exhibition of photographic art makes clear, the camera is not nature's pencil but just another species of the artist's pencil, an especially valuable tool for both art and science, but constrained by the limitations imposed on all human seeing. Any photographic image is the subject of human intervention and manipulation: in the camera, during the processes of development and printing, and finally in the manner of framing and exhibition.

EXERCISE   **If naturalism in art is not possible — as the foregoing discussion suggests — is naturalism possible in science?**

Read the fourth
portfolio *Beasts
and other illusions*

NATURAL ORDER AND SOCIAL ORDER

Earlier sections have focussed principally on two of our five original conceptions of nature: 'material world', and 'wilderness'. That is to say, they have been mainly concerned with the perception of natural objects and living things. We turn now to the question of the perception of order in nature: patterns, relationships, processes and laws which define the concept of 'natural order'. In an important sense, this order constitutes the 'meaning' we find in nature. (*Putting nature in order* takes this point further.)

In the introductory discussion of the concept of 'natural order' a distinction was made between nature and culture, between the natural environment and human activities within that environment. Such a distinction echoes the mind/body dualism, whose validity we questioned earlier. The separation of mankind and its activities from nature in the raw seems fundamental to the outlook of modern industrial societies. In the following quotation the sociologist of knowledge, Barry Barnes, describes the central importance of this separation in determining our world view:

> In highly differentiated, modern societies there is always a sharp distinction between the social and the natural. People invariably distinguish two spheres of belief, one relating to a world of objects, facts or concrete events, one to a system of values, obligations, conventions and institutional categories. Both spheres are taken for granted as permanent and valid: both, in this sense, are real. But, today, it is our construction of the natural or physical world which is the most secure and unquestioned. We appeal to nature for our basic metaphors of order and permanence ... For us, natural order is a model for understanding social order ... Whereas alternatives to our presently constructed social order are usually found threatening and dangerous, such is the confidence engendered by our conceptions of natural order that alternatives to them are merely treated as odd, or perhaps amusing. And no powerful social group or society exists with an alternative natural world view that may serve to shake our faith in our own. Quaint cosmologies in our midst, or the anthropomorphic physics of primitive societies, disturb us no more than the existence of those who believe in them. Whereas we like to think our values are best, we know our view of nature is the right one.

> Barry Barnes, *Scientific knowledge and sociological theory*, 1974

For several hundred years, European politicians debated the distinction between the 'state of nature' and the social and political state, generating in the process such important concepts as 'natural law' and 'natural rights'. Moreover, by the eighteenth century many thinkers came to believe that the natural order provided a reliable standard for judging social institutions:

> That there is a 'natural order' of things in the world, cleverly and expertly designed by God for the guidance of mankind; that the 'laws' of this natural order may be discovered by human reason; that these laws so discovered furnish a reliable and immutable standard for testing the ideas, the conduct, and the institutions of men — these were the accepted premises, the preconceptions, of most eighteenth century thinking, not only in America but also in England and France ...

Locke, more perhaps than any one else, made it possible for the eighteenth century to believe what it wanted to believe: namely, that in the world of human relations as well as in the physical world, it was possible for men to 'correspond with the general harmony of Nature'; that since man, and the mind of man, were integral parts of the work of God, it was possible for man, by the use of his mind, to bring his thought and conduct, and hence the institutions by which he lived, into a perfect harmony with the Universal Natural Order. In the eighteenth century, therefore, these truths were widely accepted as self evident: that a valid morality would be a 'natural morality', a valid religion would be a 'natural religion', a valid law of politics would be a 'natural law'.

Carl Becker, *The declaration of independence*, 1960

COMPREHENSION
QUESTION

Compare Becker's views with those of Raymond Williams in Reference 1 IN.

The anthropologist Robin Horton contrasts attitudes to 'natural order' in Western industrial societies with traditional thought in Africa where the social order is seen to be the epitome of reliability while the natural order seems much less reliable:

In complex, rapidly changing industrial societies the human scene is in flux. Order, regularity, predictability, simplicity, all these seem lamentably absent. It is in the world of inanimate things that such qualities are most readily seen. This, I suggest, is why the mind in quest of explanatory analogies turns most readily to the inanimate. In the traditional societies of Africa, we find the situation reversed. The human scene is the locus par excellence of order, predictability, regularity. In the world of the inanimate, these qualities are far less evident, and here the mind in quest of explanatory analogies turns naturally to people and their relations.

Robin Horton, 'African traditional thought and Western science', 1967

Read Reference 3 IN

In other words, whereas traditional African thinkers draw upon personal categories and social relations in order to expedite the theoretical explanation of natural events and sequences, conversely, European scientists consider physics (the most rigorously impersonal science) as the model for explanation in the biological or the social sciences.

EXERCISE

After reading Reference 3 IN, think carefully through Horton's distinction between modern European and traditional African approaches to theoretical explanation of the natural world. Before reading further on the subject, can you suggest some of the possible effects (on both African and European societies) of the different approaches to nature.

RESPONSE

Traditional Africa: Being heavily dependent on the social sphere, theoretical explanation would presumably draw heavily on such personal categories as reward and punishment, ambition, ancestors and gods. Studies of the important African intellectual traditions of witchcraft and sorcery indicate that this is so. Such considerations might help explain

Taddeo di Bartolo
St Francis' sermon to the birds, 1403
Niedersächsisches Landesmuseum, Hannover

Nature may also be approached in a sacred frame of mind. St Francis imparted full spiritual standing to the animals. Here, he exhorts the birds to praise their creator. The Franciscan view of nature sought to depose man from his special position separate from, and in domination of, the rest of 'creation'. Though he failed to revolutionise the Christian approach, it may be said that he brought to Christianity a new joy in the natural world.

why what we call 'modern science' did not develop in cultures other than that of modern Europe, and also might help us to understand why the introduction of modern science has often been so disruptive of traditional cultures.

Modern Europe: The success with which analogies from the natural world have been used in modern science has perhaps led us to apply similar analogies where they may not be appropriate: the scientific approach to ethical problems; the attempt to reduce biological explanation to physics and chemistry (called 'reductionism'); the effort to reduce sociological explanation to biology (as in the sociobiology movement); and the political and ideological use of biological explanation (as in Social Darwinism). These examples are all sometimes loosely referred to as 'scientism'.

In the following passage a Wintu Indian woman contrasts the North American Indian attitude to nature with that of the European. Notice how, in reference to nature, she chooses personalised (we might say anthropomorphic) categories in a way that may, at least in some respects, correspond to the African tribes which Horton studies, i.e. nature is explained in terms of human relations:

> The white people never cared for land or deer or bear. When we Indians kill meat, we eat it all up. When we dig roots we make little holes ... We shake down acorns and pine-nuts. We don't chop down the trees. We only use dead wood. But the white people plow up the ground, pull up the trees, kill everything. The tree says, 'Don't. I am sore. Don't hurt me.' But they chop it down and cut it up. The spirit of the land hates them. The Indians never hurt anything, but the white people destroy all. They blast rocks and scatter them on the ground. The rock says 'Don't! You are hurting me.' But the white people pay no attention. When the Indians use rocks, they take little round ones for their cooking.
>
> How can the spirit of the earth like the white man? Everywhere the white man has touched, it is sore.
>
> Theodore Roszak, *The making of the counter culture*, 1970

QUESTION
TO THINK
ABOUT

The words of the Wintu woman sound almost child-like to the ear of the modern European. Some would say her innocence reflects naivety and ignorance; others would say a greater wisdom than we have yet achieved. Consider the suggestion that many aboriginal tribal cultures maintain closer rapport with the natural world than does Western European culture?

EXERCISE

Attributing intelligence and personality to a tree or stone may be understood as a linguistic device for assigning integrity and standing. Can you think of a similar uses of language in modern European culture?

RESPONSE

'The ship sailed proudly into Sydney Harbour, saluting first the Opera House then turning her bow to the throngs gathered on Circular Quay.'

Such usage in English is confined mainly to poetic contexts. But in both examples above 'the sore tree' and 'the proud ship' the metaphor has cognitive substance, which is to say it attempts to communicate information about the real world, as well as to convey the emotive, purely subjective impressions.

Horton points to an interesting example of how the Western view of nature may sometimes impede understanding by its emphasis on the primacy of 'natural' as opposed to 'social' explanation. It has long been observed that social disorder, the breakdown of community, and hazards in the workplace account for a significant degree of human illness; both psychological and physical (if such a distinction is any longer valid). The medical profession has been slow to recognise the significance of this fact and indeed preventative health and environmental medicine still rank very low in status as medical specialties. Horton offers a possible explanation:

> Let us remind ourselves at this point that modern medical men, though long blinded to such things, are once more beginning to toy with the idea that disturbances in a person's social life can in fact contribute to a whole series of sicknesses, ranging from those commonly thought of as mental to many more commonly thought of as bodily . . .

> Modern Western medical scientists have long been distracted from noting the causal connexion between social disturbance and disease by the success of the germ theory. It would seem, indeed, that a conjunction of the germ theory, of the discovery of potent antibiotics and immunization techniques, and of conditions militating against the build-up of natural resistance to many killer infections, for long made it very difficult for scientists to see the importance of this connexion. Conversely, perhaps a conjunction of no germ theory, no potent antibiotics, no immunization techniques, with conditions favouring the build-up of considerable natural resistance to killer infections, served to throw this same causal connexion into relief in the mind of the traditional healer. If one were asked to choose between germ theory innocent of psychosomatic insight and traditional psychosomatic theory innocent of ideas about infection, one would almost certainly choose the germ theory. For in terms of quantitative results it is clearly the more vital to human well-being. But it is salutary to remember that not all the profits are on one side.

> Robin Horton, 'African traditional thought and Western science', 1967

FURTHER READING

Barry Barnes, *Scientific knowledge and sociological theory,* Routledge and Kegan Paul, London, 1974. [In his extensive discussion of the diversity of beliefs about nature, Barnes accepts much of Horton's comment about African thought but differs significantly in his interpretations of Western science.]

Mary Douglas, *Purity and danger,* Routledge and Kegan Paul, London, 1966

E. E. Evans-Pritchard, *Witchcraft, oracles and magic among the Azande,* Oxford University Press, Oxford, 1973

Robin Horton and Ruth Finnegan, *Modes of thought,* Faber and Faber, London, 1973

P. Winch, 'Understanding a primitive society', in B. Wilson (ed.), *Rationality,* Blackwell, Oxford, 1970

Not only do those of us who live in modern industrial society think of nature as ordered and predictable but we also believe our understanding of nature is uniquely valid as a way of knowing. These points are emphasised by Barry Barnes:

> ... there is an obvious rightness about our own world view. It seems, in some way, to mirror reality so straightforwardly that it must be the consequence of direct apprehension rather than effort and imagination. Conversely, alternative beliefs possess an obvious wrongness. The more natural our own perspective becomes, the more puzzling become the strange propositions of ancestors, aliens and eccentrics. How did such mistaken ideas come to be held? However have they remained uncorrected for so long? A whole series of categories exist which can be readily deployed by anyone in modern societies needing to answer such questions: inferior or impaired mentality, stupidity, prejudice, bigotry, hypocrisy, ideology, conditioning and brain-washing are but a few. All imply a distortion of what is really perceived, a disturbance of a person's normal direct apprehension of the world. Commonsense theories of the incidence of beliefs involve the actor treating his own as in need of no explanation and the varying beliefs of others as intelligible in terms of pathologies and biasing factors.
>
> Barry Barnes, *Scientific knowledge and sociological theory*, 1974

Barnes goes on to make the point that scientific theories bear socio-anthropological investigation as much as do the beliefs of a Wintu Indian or an African Shaman. In this interpretation, 'nature' is a category of thought not unlike such categories as 'culture' and 'society'. 'Nature', then, becomes neither more nor less representative of the real world, than 'culture' which is to suggest that 'nature' is not deserving of the epistemologically privileged position it has sustained in European thought. Indeed, many of the most common distinctions made between nature and culture are largely arbitrary, a point emphasised by historian David Wilson:

> Nature and its opposite, culture, are equally categorical fictions, and one of the persistent problems for members of Western cultures has been to decide which phenomena ought plausibly to be sorted into each. There is slight difficulty in assigning cathedrals to culture and foxes to nature, but certain phenomena, especially when they are new or alien to the original culture, create a kind of steady dissonance. Aboriginal Americans are an example. First, they were 'Indians', a familiar type of alien person within the cognitive map of Western culture. They were later designated 'savages', 'devils', 'animals', degenerated Jews or protohumans by those who sorted them first into piles labelled 'nature' and 'culture' and then assigned proper stations within these larger categories. The problem is that these categories are never simple, but belong to a complex of other categories that define how one is to feel, act toward or perceive objects of one category as opposed to another: one acts differently in a confrontation with a 'noble savage' than with a 'devil'.
>
> David Wilson, *In the presence of man*, 1978

EXERCISE **Taking the conception of nature as natural order, and basing your judgement on the points raised in the preceding discussion, sort out the following phenomena as 'natural' or 'cultural': forest, tree, bridge, peach, pest, homosexuality, drought, gardens, god, love and truth.**

RESPONSE My own initial response would be to put all the above phenomena into the cultural category. At the same time I can think of good reasons for classifying them all as natural. If you cannot think of individual reasons for putting each into either, you may be a more rigid thinker than you like to believe.

Your reasons for choosing one or the other category should prove most valuable in helping you tease out the cultural from the natural strands that constitute each concept. Here are some of the kinds of questions which should be considered:

Forest: How many trees constitute a forest? (Or how many hectares?) Does the concept include pine plantations? (It does in popular usage, but certainly does not in ecological or geographic terminology.) If a forest is considered an ecological system, then can one arbitrarily draw its physical boundaries? Most of the entities we call forests today have boundaries set by economic considerations of property ownership and agricultural development. They are often too small to be naturally self-sustaining, and are frequently composed of the secondary growth of a limited number of species struggling to exist in places where the natural topsoil has nearly disappeared. This outlook may be overly pessimistic about the future of forests, but it correctly emphasises the many senses in which 'natural' forests have been replaced by forest parks and plantations, entirely 'cultural' concepts.

FURTHER
READING Eric Rolls, *A million wild acres,* Nelson, 1981

Tree: An individual tree seems a safe bet for the 'nature' side. But what about a potted Norfolk pine growing in a Toronto living room? Furthermore, the classification of trees by genus and species is a process heavily influenced by cultural considerations.

Bridge: From almost any perspective, this one is 'cultural'. Yet, if one defines the concept in terms of a span of material meeting certain load-bearing requirements, then 'natural' bridges abound. In Portfolio 1, the picture of the Firth of Forth Bridge may seem to a civil engineer to portray fundamental laws of nature written across the sky.

Peach: You have probably never eaten a peach other than one of horticultural origin: the strain developed by human manipulation and the individual trees planted, pruned, protected and nourished by women and men.

Pests: Like 'pollution' and 'weed' the concept 'pest' is strictly cultural. According to

Douglas' definition 'matter out of place', objects (living or inanimate) are so defined whenever they interfere with human activities or goals, e.g. oil on a beach, a petunia in an onion patch, a cockatoo in a field of grain.

FURTHER
READING

Mary Douglas, *Purity and danger*, Routledge and Kegan Paul, London, 1966
David Wade Chambers, *Worm in the bud*, Deakin University, Waurn Ponds, revd edn 1984

Homosexuality: Whether homosexual behaviour is judged natural or unnatural will be strongly influenced by the prevailing attitude in a society. Certainly there have been gay people in all human societies however tolerant or oppressive, and homosexual behaviour is exhibited by many animal species in their native environment. Beneath the negative emotional and moral connotations conveyed by the accusation that homosexuality is unnatural lies the claim that it is contrary to the biological order of nature. According to one (non-theological) version of this argument, since homosexuals do not have children, their sexual practices thwart natural selection (and, therefore, must be learned rather than inherited). Against this idea must be set the evidence that many people who are homosexually active bear and father children. Moreover, it may be argued that homosexuality operates as a form of population control in a number of species, including human beings. The sociobiologist, Edward O. Wilson, has recently proposed a controversial mechanism to explain how a propensity for homosexual behaviour might be inherited. He suggests that if the resources homosexuals do not expend on children of their own are devoted to the offspring of their close relatives, then those relatives might be able to rear more children to reproductive age.

FURTHER
READING

Edward O. Wilson, *On human nature*, Bantam, New York, 1979, esp. pp. 147–154
Doug Futuyama, 'Is there a gay gene? Does it matter?', *Science for the people*, vol. 12, 1980, pp. 10–15
John Boswell, *Christianity, social tolerance and homosexuality*, University of Chicago Press, Chicago, 1981

Drought: At first glance, this might seem to be entirely 'natural'. Yet, the perception of drought is extremely subjective and directly related to the degree of economic significance of the water shortage.

FURTHER
READING

R. L. Heathcote, 'Drought in Australia: a problem of perception', *The geographical review*, vol. 59, April 1969, pp. 175–194

Gardens: To design and maintain a garden requires considerable knowledge of nature, and some garden styles attempt to simulate a natural environment. Nevertheless, gardens are ultimately human fabrications more akin to houses and buildings than to the works of nature—though the garden of Eden might be thought of as 'supernatural'.

God, love and truth: These concepts are perhaps radically different from others in the list, but can you distinguish both natural and cultural components in these ideas?

The objective of this exercise is not, of course, to discover the 'correct' categories, but rather to indicate how closely bound together are the ideas of nature and culture, how difficult, and finally pointless it may be to disentangle them. There are several dangers in this conflation. In my experience, most people tend to class most of the above as natural. And since in our society the things of nature partake of the status of 'facts', their cultural derivation may often be forgotten. David Wilson indicated in the passage quoted above how this may affect our perception of race, for instance. It also seems likely that wrongly assessing the natural and social components of decisions relating to the environment may be responsible for the ecological crises we presently face. Can you think of further examples?

In what sense then, I ask again, do we perceive the natural order? As with all other seeing, the answer is through cultural, psychological and biological lenses. Reference 2 IN vividly suggests some of the cultural parameters which may affect the way we see nature.

One particularly fruitful area of anthropological research has explored the various ways different cultures divide and classify things in nature. In some measure, natural boundaries, natural kinds and species are artificial constructs reflecting cultural as much as scientific interests. This view is associated with Ernest Cassirer, Edward Sapir and Benjamin Lee Whorf. Whorf remarked:

See *Putting nature in order,* Exhibit 6

> We cut nature up, organise it into concepts, and ascribe significances as we do, largely because we are parties to an agreement to organise it this way—an agreement that holds throughout our speech community and is codified in the patterns of our language ... We are thus introduced to a new principle of relativity, which holds that all observers are not led by the same physical evidence to the same picture of the universe ... The real question is: what do different languages do ... with the flowing face of nature in its motion, color, and changing form? For, as goes our signification of the face of nature, so goes our physics of the cosmos.
>
> J. B. Carroll (ed.), *Language, thought and reality: selected writings of Benjamin Lee Whorf,* 1956

Over the years, the Whorf thesis has passed in and out of favour, but whatever one may feel about his particular views of language, Whorf's ideas remain a forceful and provocative account of cultural relativism.

FURTHER
READING

John B. Carroll (ed.), *Language, thought and reality: Selected writings of Benjamin Lee Whorf,* MIT Press, Cambridge, Mass., 1956
Ernest Cassirer, *Language and myth,* Dover, New York, 1953

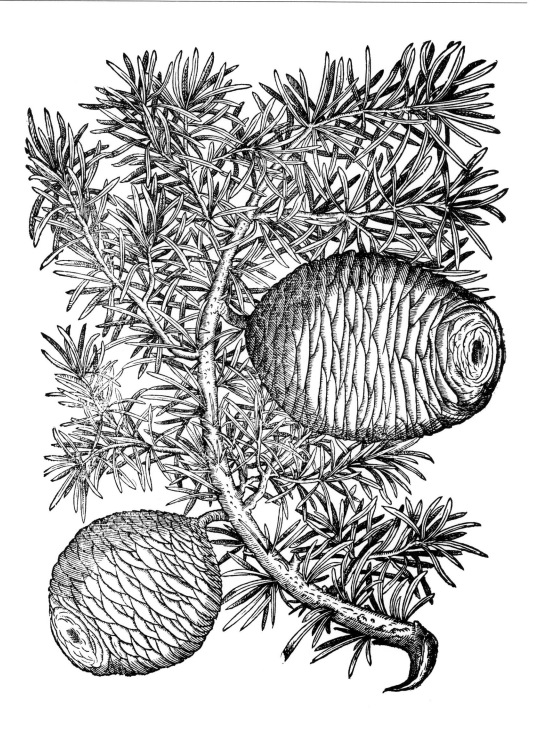

J. B. Deregowski, *Illusions, patterns and pictures: a cross-cultural perspective*, Academic Press, 1980

G. A. Miller and P. N. Johnson-Laird, *Language and perception*, Harvard University Press, Cambridge, Mass., 1976

Edward Sapir, *Culture, language and personality: selected essays*, University of California Press, Berkeley, 1949

M. H. Segall, D. T. Campbell and M. T. Herskovits, *The influences of culture on visual perception*, Bobbs-Merrill, New York, 1966

I have found it helpful to think of the process of seeing nature as analogous to what the art theorist Rudolph Arnheim has (with special reference to painters) called 'visual thinking'. He says:

> It must be realized that an artist's most important way of working through the problem of existence is by means of the images he invents, judges, and manipulates. When such an image reaches its final state he perceives in it the outcome of his visual thinking. He knows now what he was struggling to clarify. A work of visual art, in other words, is not an illustration of the thoughts of its maker, but rather the final manifestation of that thinking itself.
>
> Rudolph Arnheim, *Visual thinking*, 1965

Whenever we form images of nature even in the simple sensory event of looking at a stream in a country landscape, we might be said to be working through a problem similar to that of a painter with his easel. Although our final image is not recorded on canvas, it may nevertheless be recorded.

Eventually the process of evoking this remembered image may come to supplant the actual process of seeing. Thus, there may be a grim truth in the comment by the former governor of California and President of the U.S.A., Ronald Reagan, 'When you've seen one tree, you've seen them all.'

Some time ago, I walked across an Australian coastal heathland which was being considered for development by the Shire Council. In this open woodland, in sight of the sea, carpets of orchids and other wildflowers were in bloom. And on that particular day, I saw for the first time the exotic Southern Emu Wren. There were parrots and other fine native birds, kangaroos and wallabies, and no doubt snakes and beetles and all manner of creatures for those who would take the time to see. I should like to have seen this spot through the 'expert eyes' of a naturalist or aboriginal bushman.

In the Shire records is enshrined the perception of the dentist who owned the land and wanted to 'improve' it. 'After all', he said, 'scrub is scrub'.

This story shows, I think, how our 'visual thinking' may ossify; our visual hypotheses

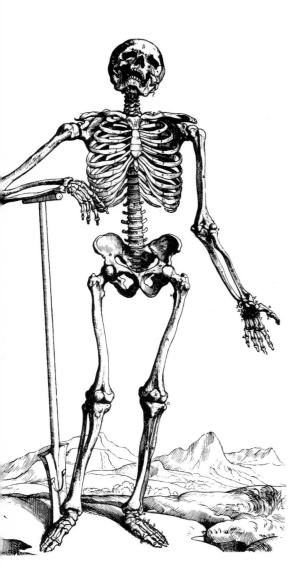

may become 'facts' as hard and dead as bones in a desert. Living images, normally subject to renewal and revision, may become stereotyped representations of the natural environment. Such seeing is more akin to belief than to perception.

In examining this concept 'natural order', we quickly became aware of how many cultural contingencies influence the judgement of what is natural and what is not, of what is ordered and what is not. Cultural tradition is the mortar of nature. Coherent perspectives of natural order are held together by the sacred repetitions of traditional belief and ceremonial usage. This is true not only in tribal societies but also in the vast industrial complexes of the modern world. We are all, tribal and modern, of a mentality akin to that of one of Piaget's little boys, who declared that the moon could not be called 'sun', nor the sun 'moon', 'because the moon must be the moon and not the sun and the sun must be the sun.' In other words, we cling to our understanding of nature because from earliest childhood we are taught the formulae which will eventually structure our thought processes and determine our seeing.

Even our scientists, as Thomas Kuhn has suggested, are loath to give up those paradigmatic theories of nature which they absorb in coming to scientific literacy. Is it true, then, that science offers us the best hope of transcending both tribal and modern 'dreamtime' images of nature?

Undoubtedly, science, as we observed earlier, is instrumentally progressive. It enables us to do things we could not have done before. And in that fact there is a basis for both hope and despair.

The despair comes from the economic associations of science, which may tie its seeing to particular forms of political interest and ambition.

The hope derives from a re-evaluation of older ways of understanding the scientific enterprise, which align it more closely with the world of art and free inquiry than with the world of economic and military 'necessity'. Perhaps such a science would be humble, more democratic, more flexible, more eclectic, and altogether more effective in improving our understanding of nature than is the science of today. With such a science, we might imagine a new heaven and a new earth.

Gustav Courbet
The artist on the seashore at Palavas, 1854
Musée Fabre, Montpellier; Edimedia

The artist salutes nature as he would render homage
to his liege passing in parade, yet there is in the
man's stance a quality of self-assertion and pride.

BIBLIOGRAPHY

Rudolph Arnheim, *Visual thinking*, University of California Press, Berkeley, 1965

Barry Barnes, *Scientific knowledge and sociological theory*, Routledge and Kegan Paul, London, 1974

Carl Becker, *The declaration of independence*, Knopf, New York, 1960

Jonathon Benthall (ed.), *Ecology, the shaping enquiry*, Longman, London, 1972

George Berkeley, *The theory of vision vindicated*, London, 1733

C. M. Bloomer, *Principles of visual perception*, Van Nostrand Reinhold, New York, 1976.

John Boswell, *Chistianity, social tolerance and homosexuality*, University of Chicago Press, Chicago, 1981.

Iain Cameron, *Metaphor in science and society*, Siscon Project, Manchester University, Manchester, 1976

John V. Canfield and Franklin H. Donnell, *Readings in the theory of knowledge*, Appleton Century Crofts, New York, 1964

John B. Carroll (ed.), *Language, thought and reality: selected Writings of Benjamin Lee Whorf*, MIT Press, Cambridge, Mass., 1956

Ernest Cassirer, *Language and myth*, Dover, New York, 1953

Allan Chalmers, *What is this thing called science?*, Queensland University Press, Brisbane, 1979

David Wade Chambers, *On the social analysis of science*, Deakin University, Waurn Ponds, 1979

David Wade Chambers, *Liberation and control*, Deakin University, Waurn Ponds, 1979

David Wade Chambers, *Worm in the bud*, Deakin University, Waurn Ponds, 1979

R. G. Collingwood, *The idea of nature*, Clarendon Press, Oxford, 1965

J. B. Deregowski, *Illusions, patterns and pictures: a cross-cultural perspective*, Academic Press, 1980.

Mary Douglas, *Purity and danger*, Routledge and Kegan Paul, London, 1966

Vitus Droscher, *The magic of the senses*, Dutton, New York, 1969

Pierre Duhem, *The aim and structure of physical theory*, Princeton University Press, Princeton, 1954

Rene Dubos, *The dreams of reason*, Columbia University Press, New York, 1961

E. E. Evans-Pritchard, *Witchcraft, oracles and magic among the Azande*, Oxford University Press, Oxford, 1973

Lyndsay Farrall, *Nature and social power*, Deakin University, Waurn Ponds, 1982

Roger Fry, *Reflections on British painting*, London, 1934

Doug Futuyama, 'Is there a gay gene? Does it matter?', *Science for the people*, vol. 12, 1980, pp. 10–15

J. J. Gibson, *The perception of the visual world*, Houghton Mifflin, Boston, 1950

Clarence H. Glacken, *Traces on a Rhodian shore*, University of California Press, Berkeley, 1973

E. H. Gombrich, *Art and illusion*, Phaidon Press, London, 1960

Stephen Jay Gould, *The mismeasure of man*, Norton, New York, 1981

R. L. Gregory, *Concepts and mechanisms of perception*, Scribner's Sons, New York, 1974

R. L. Gregory and E. H. Gombrich (eds.), *Illusion in nature and art*, Duckworth, London, 1973

N. R. Hanson, *Patterns of discovery*, Cambridge University Press, Cambridge, U. K., 1958

N. R. Hanson, *Perception and discovery*, Freeman-Cooper, San Francisco, 1969

R. L. Heathcote, 'Drought in Australia: a problem of perception', *Geographical review*, vol. 59, April 1969, pp. 175–194

Robin Horton, 'African traditional thought and Western science', *Africa*, vol. 67, pp. 50–71 and 175–194

Robin Horton and Ruth Finnegan, *Modes of thought*, Faber and Faber, London, 1973

Liam Hudson, *The cult of the fact*, Jonathan Cape, London, 1972

Struan Jacobs, *On the philosophical analysis of science*, Deakin University, Waurn Ponds, 1979

T. S. Kuhn, *The structure of scientific revolutions*, University of Chicago Press, Chicago, 1970

T. S. Kuhn, *The essential tension*, University of Chicago Press, Chicago, 1977

William Leiss, *The domination of nature*, George Braziller, New York, 1972

C. R. Leslie, *Memoirs of the life of John Constable*, London, 1843

Arthur O. Lovejoy, *The great chain of being*, Harvard University Press, Cambridge, Mass., 1964

E. Lucie-Smith, *The invented eye*, Paddington, New York, 1975

P. K. Machamer and R. G. Turnbull (eds.), *Studies in perception*, Ohio State University, Columbus, 1978

Herbert Marcuse, *One dimensional man*, Beacon Press, Boston, 1964

G. A. Miller and P. N. Johnson-Laird, *Language and perception*, Harvard University Press, Cambridge, Mass., 1976

Eadweard Muybridge, *Animals in motion*, Dover, New York, 1957

M. J. Morgan, *Molyneux's question*, Cambridge University Press, Cambridge, U. K., 1977

Nicholas Pastore, *Selective history of theories of visual perception: 1650–1950*, Oxford University Press, Oxford, 1971

Michael Polanyi, *Personal knowledge*, Routledge and Kegan Paul, London, 1973

Karl R. Popper, *The logic of scientific discovery*, Hutchinson, London, 1959

Karl R. Popper, *Conjectures and refutations*, Routledge and Kegan Paul, London, 1972

H. H. Price, *Perception*, Methuen, London, 1932

Eric Rolls, *A million wild acres*, Nelson, Melbourne, 1981

Theodore Roszak, *The making of the counter culture*, Faber and Faber, London, 1970

John Ruskin, *The elements of drawing*, London, 1857

Edward Sapir, *Culture, language and personality: selected essays*, University of California Press, Berkeley, 1949

Marshall H. Segall, Donald T. Campbell and Melville J. Herskovits, *The influence of culture on visual perception*, Bobbs-Merrill, New York, 1966

William H. Fox Talbot, *The pencil of nature*, 1844

Stephen Toulmin, *The philosophy of science: An Introduction*, Hutchinson, London, 1953

Colin M. Turnbull, *The forest people*, Simon and Schuster, New York, 1961

Godfrey Vasey, *Perception*, Open University Press, 1973

Lynn White Jr., *Machina ex deo*, MIT Press, Cambridge, Mass., 1968

Basil Willey, *The eighteenth century background: studies on the idea of nature in the thought of the period*, Chatto and Windus, London, 1967

David Wilson, *In the presence of nature*, University of Massachusetts, Amherst, 1978

Edward O. Wilson, *On human nature*, Bantam, New York, 1979

P. Winch, 'Understanding a primitive society', in B. Wilson (ed.), *Rationality*, Blackwell, Oxford, 1970

Richard Wollheim, 'Reflections on art and illusion', in Richard Wollheim, *On Art and mind, Essays and lectures*, Allen Lane, London, 1973, pp. 261–289

ACKNOWLEDGEMENTS

Black-and-white illustrations

Facing imprint page, from Hieronymus Rodler, *Eyn schön nütlich büchlin*, Siemern, 1531, Houghton Library, Harvard University; contents page, pp. 4, 6, 13, 44, 49, woodcuts from *Commentaries on the Six Books of Dioscorides*, Venice, 1563 and Prague, 1565, by Pierandrea Mattioli, in *Herbal*, by Joseph Wood Crutch, Balance House, New York, 1965; p. 1, from *De Historia Stirpum*, by Fuchs, in *The Illustrated Herbal*, by Wilfrid Blunt and Sandra Raphael, Thames and Hudson in association with the Metropolitan Museum of Art, 1979; pp. 3, 7, 8, 10, 18, 26, 34, 35, 43, from *1800 Woodcuts by Thomas Bewick and his school*, ed. Blanche Cirker, Dover Publications, New York, 1962; p. 11, from *Hart Picture Archives: Compendium*, Hart Publishing Co., New York; p. 15, from Descartes' *Dioptrique*, 1637; pp. 20, 51, from Andreas Vesalius, *De humani corporis fabrica*, 1543, p. 23, from Descartes' *L'homme*, 1661; p. 26 (visual illusion), from *The Art and Science of Visual Illusions*, by Nicholas Wade, Routledge & Kegan Paul, 1982; p. 29, from *Sex in the Garden*, ed. Tom Riker, William Morrow & Co., Inc., New York, n.d.; p. 38, from *Hortus Sanitatis*, by Johann Meydenbach, in the catalogue for the exhibition entitled Renaissance Books of Science From the Collection of Albert E. Lownes, Dartmouth College, Hanover, New Hampshire, 1970.

Cover

Flight, 1916, woodcut by E. McKnight Kauffer, courtesy Victoria and Albert Museum, London.